Jobs – Careers For Masters and Doctoral Graduates

HOW TO CREATE THE INCOME AND LIFESTYLE YOU WANT

William G. Wargo, Ph.D
Patricia V. Tobin, Ph. D

Verus Press
New York

Jobs – Careers For Masters and Doctoral Graduates
Copyright © William G. Wargo and Patricia V. Tobin

All rights are reserved. There is no part of this publication that may be reproduced in any form or manner, distributed, or transmitted in any form or by any other means, including but not limited to photocopying, recording, or any other electronic or mechanical methods, without the prior written permission of the publisher, except in the case of brief quotations embodied in critical reviews and certain other noncommercial uses permitted by copyright law. For permission requests, please, write to the publisher, at the address below.

Disclaimer

The information offered by the authors and publisher is intended to provide education and general career guidance. Nothing in this book or the website listed, or during a regular career consultation, guarantees employment. The purpose and general goal of this career guidance offered by the authors is to educate, inspire, and encourage the reader about their career choices.

Verus Press
1552 5th Avenue

Watervliet, NY, 12189

First Edition, 2020

ISBN: 978-1-944772-02-4
Printed in the United States of America

New York

DEDICATIONS

To my wife, Liz; To my daughter, Sherrie; To my son, Jason.

– WGW

I dedicate this book to my husband Darrin and son Connor.

– PVT

Foreword

It is a great honor to publish the book "Jobs-Careers for Masters & Doctoral Graduates" posthumously for my late husband Dr. William Wargo. Dr. Wargo was a much admired and respected scholar whose life work included counseling, teaching and academic guidance specializing in dissertation completion. He was the founder and director of The Academic Information Center and author of "Secrets and Tips of Dissertation Completion." Dr. Wargo was a remarkable man and will be greatly missed.

Elizabeth Wargo

Acknowledgements

With the birth of this book- and that's what this is: a birthing, a creating, and ultimately a publishing, there are so many wonderful people to thank. Firstly, I thank God for inspiring me so that somehow the message I have brought to this book is pure and helpful to you the reader. I thank Patricia Tobin, my co-author, for her willingness to partner with me on this venture. Our weekly conferences have made a huge difference for me. I thank Jeffry Evans for his encouragement to write more about what I know, 1st on our website and then in this book. I thank my wife, Liz, for always encouraging me and discussing the many ideas I had for this book. I thank the hundreds of individuals I have met over the years who have shared with me their hopes and dreams for their right job or career, for their way of finding their life's work. There are so many of you and I am forever grateful for your willingness to tell me of your frustrations and successes. All of you are in some way included someplace in this book.

– WGW

The completion of this book would not have been possible without the encouragement and assistance of so many people. I would like to thank the following people: my husband Darrin, son Connor for their continuous love and support for my academic endeavors and teaching career over so many years; my father Dr.

Fernando Venecia for providing the love and support throughout my life; my grandmother Sara Garza Venecia who was a teaching role model, and my sister Priscilla and her husband Dr. Rudolf Tomanik for their love and positive influence over the years.

I thank Dr. William Wargo who is my co–author, mentor, colleague and friend, and Professor Nancy Zeller for her friendship, guidance and creative inspiration on the development of the book.

Lastly, I am grateful to my wonderful colleagues I have known at the different higher education institutions who have provided insights about their own job hunting. This book could not have been completed without them.

– PVT

Contents

Dedication	3
Foreword	4
Acknowledgements	5
Introduction: Our Vision for this Book	9
Chapter 2: The World of Work in America in the 21st Century	27
Chapter 3: All About Me	39
Chapter 4: Attitudes for Success	51
Chapter 5: Maximizing Yourself	57
Chapter 6: What Jobs/Careers Are Out There?	63
Chapter 7: Be Strategic About Your Job Search	67
Chapter 8: Interviewing Tips	73
Chapter 9: Tips for an Impressive Resume/Vita	81
Chapter 10: Networking	95
Chapter 11: Concluding Reflections	107
Afterwords: Applying What You Learned	115
About the Author, Dr. William Wargo	117
About the Author, Dr. Patricia Tobin	118

INTRODUCTION

OUR VISION FOR THIS BOOK

The aphorism, "As a man thinketh in his heart so is he," not only embraces the whole of a man's being, but is so comprehensive as to reach out to every condition and circumstance of his life. A man is literally what he thinks, his character being the complete sum of all his thoughts.

— James Allen, *As A Man Thinketh*

"Musicians must make music, artists must paint, poets must write, if they are to be ultimately at peace with themselves. What humans can be, they must be. They must be true to their own nature."

— Abraham Maslow

What is Your Commitment to Getting the Income and Lifestyle You Want?

WHEN YOU THINK about the time commitment that was required to earn a masters degree it was probably something like this: a 12 course M.A. or M.S. degree at 40 hours per course comes to 480 hours of class time. If one assumes that it takes at least one hour for study and preparation for every hour in class, that's another 480 hours for a grand total of 960 hours devoted to earning the masters degree. For this example… Some doctoral degrees take at least twice as long, which would be 1,920 hours. We believe these numbers are somewhat conservative. As you read this book, you already have either or both of these degrees, so you have experienced the tremendous time and effort it takes for the completion of your degree(s).

How much time are you willing to commit to obtaining the income and lifestyle you long for? As you will see later in this book, we make it clear that you have many skills, abilities, and special knowledge that collectively any employer, any business or any endeavor would desperately desire in a new associate. The only thing you would need to do at this point, is to become serious about investigating the multiple possibilities available to you so that you can reach your goal of financial security and more happiness.

Whether you are employed now or not, you are reading this book because you are interested in improving your situation. Now would be the moment to consider devoting a certain amount of time per day or per week to investigate, to contact, to apply, and to follow up on legitimate possibilities for yourself. Do continual research.

Remember: most people find their jobs or careers by accident – not on purpose. That is not what you want to do.

Circumstances played a major role in their final occupational landing. This is the major reason so many men and women find themselves unhappy with their work-a-day life. For many, it is only after years of dealing with difficult and unfulfilling employment, that some go after what they really want to do. You may have heard it said: **people either have plenty of time, but not enough money - or - they have "all the money in the world," but not enough time to enjoy it.** It is possible to have the amount of free time you want as well as the income to afford the things you desire. **It takes research planning and action.**

This book was written for masters and/or doctoral graduates who want a better income and lifestyle. If you hold either or both of these degrees, then what you are about to read will have profound meaning for your job or career plans. Those of you with advanced degrees need to understand that the expectations on the job are increasing at a fast pace. Let us give you an example from the field of nursing. Not too long ago, a person could receive nursing training at a hospital and receive a diploma in Nursing. After passing a state examination, one could become a Registered Nurse. There were two other options: an Associate Degree in Nursing and a Bachelor of Science Degree in Nursing (BSN). With either of these degrees and successfully passing the state nursing examination, one would qualify to become a Registered Nurse. Now things are changing. As reported in *The Wall Street Journal,* Anna Louie Sussman and Melissa Korn claim that despite the critical shortage of nurses, many hospitals are refusing to hire registered nurses with only a nursing diploma or associate degree in nursing. The argument for only hiring BSN graduates is that these individuals have additional training in: "community health, critical thinking, and evaluating research, in addition to general education classes." So where does it stop? Are there other career fields where only a bachelor's degree is not enough? More education and training seem to be the expectation in most fields. **And you have an advanced degree, a masters and/or a doctorate.**

Assuming that experience is about the same and interviewing skills are about the same, the difference in who gets hired may very well be those who have training and experience beyond the minimum.

Various research studies indicate that up to 80% of all working people in America are unhappy with many aspects of their job or career. When you include the "unemployed" individuals with the "under-employed" and the "mis-employed," over 90% of the eligible total work-force in the country are dissatisfied with their work. This data makes a significant statement about the concept of work as a necessary evil justified only by the need to make money. It illustrates the fact that many people have forgotten or never learned that work needs to be more than just a means of earning a livelihood. To be truly satisfying, work must give expression to the highest potential within the individual. This is what Abraham Maslow, Ph.D. conveys in his book, *A Theory of Human Motivation*, called "self-actualization." Work needs to be an opportunity for continued learning and growth, for without this there is a stagnation of life and a festering of boredom, frustration, hopelessness, and unhappiness.

Job Hunting Mentality

You will want to change your approach regarding the process of finding your best job or career. It is an ongoing cluster of activities, which includes understanding yourself and understanding the opportunities in the marketplace. You may have heard of this: **Necessity is the Mother of Invention.** It is very appropriate when one considers the sense of urgency in locating a new job. If the urgency is high, then the efforts to locate a job should be maximized. If one is already employed and considering other options that may be better than what they have, then the process can be much more systematic and long-term. One would have the time to carefully consider many choices. I (William) recall a time when I was center director of a small education center for a Christian college in San Diego. We offered four bachelor degrees and one masters degree. Occasionally, someone would come into the office without an appointment wanting to apply to teach at our Center. Of course, they had their vita ready and had teaching experience at other locations. Some had masters degrees and others had doctorates. After talking with them for a while, I was somewhat amazed that they had only been in town for a few days and were now scouring all opportunities throughout San Diego County for teaching positions. For these individuals it was critical that they secured employment as fast as possible. Although San Diego State, University of California San Diego, University of San Diego, and numerous community colleges were scattered throughout the county, they found our small Education Center. These employment seekers were looking anywhere and everywhere for teaching jobs because they needed the income right away. And they found us.

On the other extreme of job/career searching, my friend Ed is a good example. He was employed as a mid-level administrator at a local school district. The pay was good; the benefits were adequate; he liked his work and he always was pursuing other job/career options. This was in the day when there was no Internet and no email. He located job announcements from newspapers, newsletters, and postings on bulletin boards at various places. He also did a great job of networking. When I talked to Ed, he almost always would ask about personnel changes, retirements, and possible new programs that were being developed. He was always searching for new opportunities and he always had an up-to-date vita available. So what job hunting mentality do you have? Are you in a crisis mode and must find a job as soon as possible? Are you currently employed, but are unsure that you want to stay in your present position, but you're open to new options? The right mental approach is the way to maximize all your efforts to find a job/career you want.

Common Attributes, Characteristics, and Competencies of Those with Advanced Degrees

You may not have all of these, but we are confident you have many of these attributes, characteristics, and competencies to offer in any endeavor. You may want to read through these and do a brief self-assessment to identify those you feel are a part of your makeup.

- **CRITICAL THINKING:** This is what Julian Meltzoff writes about in *Critical Thinking About Research: Psychology and Related Fields.* He states: "The phrase (critical thinking) refers to the skill that one has in thinking about an issue, analyzing it, looking at it from all sides, and weighing whether there is sufficient evidence of good-enough quality to warrant making a reasoned judgment that is as free of personal bias as possible." What organization would love to have more employees with this talent? Could you use critical thinking to starting a business of your own?

- **EVALUATION OF RESEARCH:** At every level and at every organization, research is constantly being done on a day-to-day basis. Evaluations are made such as: something as simple as analyzing daily sales figures, the effectiveness of advertising campaigns, or deciding which candidate from a group of applicants is the best one to hire. The larger the company and organization, the more in-depth the research becomes. To a greater or lesser degree you have been evaluating research, no doubt mostly from research articles, but you do understand the fundamentals of research you learned in your academic studies. These research basics can be applied to yourself.

- **HIGH READING LEVEL:** There is no doubt that in order to complete advanced degrees you had excellent reading skills. These reading skills are vitally important in the employment world since reports require an excellent reading acuity.

- **INSIGHTFUL COMPREHENSION:** So often we take courses that have cross over influence; what we learned in one course can directly or indirectly influence what were learning in a new course. The more we study in advanced learning, the more we understand that there is a great integration of knowledge and this gives us new insights that impact our comprehension.

- **EXCELLENT CONCENTRATION:** Learning in advanced courses requires focused concentration because you are always being asked to describe the content as well as how that content affects the professor's questions. This means you have focus. It is important to block out interruptions that could distract you from finishing the task of learning.

- **DELAYED GRATIFICATION:** Earning graduate degrees requires much effort, focus, and time. Most graduate degrees take from two years to six years or more. One is certainly delaying the wonderful gratification of earning the degree.

- **PATIENCE:** This characteristic is very much in alignment with the previous one, delayed gratification. Graduate courses take anywhere from 8 to 15 weeks to complete and then there's the waiting for the grade. Nothing is instantaneous.

- **FOLLOW THROUGH:** Completing an advanced degree requires great effort at meeting course requirements including writing term papers, reading assignments, and preparing and passing examinations. All of this is done over numerous semesters, and for the doctorate over number of years.

- **GLOBAL KNOWLEDGE:** The context of term papers, theses, and dissertations are always written with some aspect of the larger view beyond just the academic discipline. These writing tasks must be put into a larger context which may include an international worldview. Most research papers start with a statement of the problem which gives the impetus for the purpose of the study. Although this is not always the case, it is frequently true.

- **INTEGRATION OF KNOWLEDGE:** In the world of work combining information and knowledge from various sources is becoming a more and more critical aspect of success on the job. Individuals with advanced education are taught to integrate knowledge in almost all of their research papers as well as on comprehensive examinations.

- **SPECIALIZED KNOWLEDGE:** Most masters and doctoral degrees are specialized by definition. For instance, there are advanced degrees in school counseling, advertising, marketing, civil engineering, to name a few. Many times, these specialized programs offer internships and practicums on the job as part of the degree program so that the student, in addition to theory, gets practical experience on the job.

- **LEADERSHIP SKILLS:** Numerous universities now offer graduate degree programs in educational and business leadership. Again, most of these programs have incorporated on-the-job experiences that are integrated into the curriculum. Students are meeting with corporate leaders at all levels and sitting in on planning sessions.

- **LIFELONG LEARNING VALUES:** About 30 years ago the University of California, Riverside started a continuing education division in which they used the promotional phrase, "lifelong learning." This concept has now been accepted throughout graduate programs in the country. Many programs offer postdoctoral advanced training in many specialized fields. In Connecticut, a few of the universities offer what is known as a Certificate of Advanced Graduate Study. Most of these programs are totally integrated into the students prior work experience.

- **INITIATIVE:** To be successful in graduate school one certainly needs to get in the habit of taking the initiative. That can take the form of specific courses you choose to take; deciding on the topics for the numerous research papers that had to be written; and the willingness to participate in classroom dialogue to name a few. All of these and other activities required you to take a risk and get involved, to be pro-active.

- **ACTION-ORIENTED:** In order to succeed in graduate school, where most of the courses are so caught in a seminar format, being proactive in taking the lead in the various projects that are assigned, required you to take action. In many larger classes students were grouped into 3 or 4 students to do research and make presentations to the class. Almost always one individual becomes a spokesperson to coordinate the presentation. That was probably you.

- **EXCELLENT COMMUNICATION SKILLS:** This could be the most important skill you learned and developed in your graduate studies. If you recall, almost every course required you to give one or more verbal reports and no doubt a few written papers. Both of these activities were evaluated and graded by your professor and you had to score a grade of "A" or "B" in order to successfully pass the course. Frequently, the oral reports you presented included a question and answer session. During this time, you had to articulate in-depth when needed the strengths and weaknesses of the topic you had just finished presenting. And you had to do this in front of your peers, who were not always gentle with their comments and questions. The important thing here to remember is that you were able to critically and spontaneously respond in an impressive way. The term papers you wrote required a high level of proficiency, logical organization, adequate research, and acceptable conclusions. Therefore, you have clear evidence of your excellent communication skills. All employers expect this from their employees. If you choose to move toward self-employment of any kind, you will be able to rely on these oral and written communication talents as you interact with customers and/or clients.

- **FOCUSED LEARNING:** In a book by Frederick Evers, James Roche, and Iris Berdrow entitled *The Bases of Competence: Skills for Lifelong Learning and Employability,* they presented what can be considered the foundations of competence. These include: (1) managing yourself, (2) communicating, (3) managing other people and tasks, and (4) mobilizing innovation and change. To manage yourself, one needs to constantly be developing and practicing routines to maximize one's ability. Communicating involves interacting with individuals and groups to facilitate maximum effectiveness. Managing individuals and projects requires planning, organizing, coordinating, and controlling resources. To activate innovation and change necessitates conceptualizing ways of initiating and managing change as it constantly evolves. How many of these do you have?

So why does the overwhelming majority of the population choose to be unhappy in their work? The key word in this question is "choose." Darren Hardy in *The Compound Effect: Multiplying Your Success One Step At A Time*, delivers a profound concept that it is our choices, good or bad, conscious or unconscious, that bring us to this present place or situation in our lives. Most people have a great degree of control when deciding on their job/career. Or do they? Consider the circumstances behind the "choosing" of your work. In spite of apparent free will, many people seem to fall into a job quite by accident. You were looking and it was available; therefore it must be for you. Sometimes subtle pressures from parents or friends push you into "approved" work world positions. Or perhaps the values of society make some professions more acceptable than others. Often comments about your "limitations" keep you from the awareness of your many talents and capabilities. For others, the fantasized vision of a particular job draws you to it, but it's reality that makes you feel misplaced. Unfortunately, the outer-directed influences are often stronger than the our inner sense of our own needs and preferences. And it is often difficult to break these ties because they represent links to the past and to security. It may be difficult to let go of an idea of a particular job/career you thought was so important (especially when it required a significant investment of time, money, and preparation – your masters or doctoral degree).

But sometimes, when discomfort becomes greater than the feeling of security, people do let go. Often they seek professional help because their own previous efforts did not produce satisfying results. Traditional career counseling offers a barrage of tests which supposedly gather statistical information for funneling an individual's skills and interests into the proper line of work. Once the right niche has been discovered, the individual is shown how to fit into the mold of that organization. Using role-playing techniques, the do's and don'ts of interviewing are practiced and the individual is taught the right way to talk, act, and look. The concept of "saying what the employer wants to hear" becomes the key to success and the means to gainful employment. Sometimes these career consulting organizations even pave the way for their polished graduates by making contacts with potential employers who are seeking "the right kind" of employee.

How could such an objective approach ever fail? And yet, too often these employees end up feeling they are right back where they started – dissatisfied, misplaced, unhappy, and unfulfilled. It would seem that traditional career consulting and coaching overlooks the key ingredient in the creation of the ideal job – that is, your uniqueness. It is the subjective elements of your behaviors, attitudes, and experiences which goes into making your life what it is today. Unless these are considered in an analysis of the job/career which is right for you, results will be less than satisfying. It is more important to ask yourself what you want and like rather than what the organization wants. It is more important to encourage the expression of your uniqueness than to determine how you can be made to fit the structure of the position.

Dr. Tim's Story

Dr. Tim is a good example of someone who was very creative in applying his doctoral degree in the teaching field. After graduating with his Ph.D. in psychology, he applied to teach at a number of schools in San Diego County. By the end of the Summer after his graduation, he had secured adjunct teaching assignments at Mesa College, San Diego City College, Chapman College, and San Diego State University. He did a wonderful job of meeting the administrators at each of those schools and letting them know his preferences for days and times to teach. So with some adroit scheduling, he was able to teach morning classes at the community colleges and evening classes at Chapman and San Diego State. Dr. Tim was very effective in networking with the schedulers at these four schools. At the time I (William) was an administrator for an off-campus program with Chapman College, now Chapman University. He continued to teach at these colleges for a number of years. Eventually he relocated back to his home city of New York, where he was hired as a professor at the State University of New York.

One thing I always admired about Dr. Tim was that two years prior to graduating with his doctorate, he had already applied to numerous schools throughout the San Diego County. He was teaching various courses sporadically at a total of six different schools. He was constantly expanding and reinforcing his network. I know because he stopped by my center occasionally just to say "hi" and to remind me that he was available to teach. He even suggested certain courses he could teach in which he had an extra strong academic background. I liked the fact that he brought to my attention courses that he was teaching at other schools. He asked me if we had a similar course that he might teach. Dr. Tim epitomizes the **application of two fundamental concepts:**

preparation and networking, which made a big difference in obtaining the job or career that he wanted. First, he did early preparation by securing part-time teaching positions at various schools before he graduated with this doctorate. He already established an excellent reputation with the individuals who did the hiring. Second, he had a comprehensive networking approach by visiting the administrators who scheduled courses at the schools to just check-in with them. This contributed to having a friendly relationship so that when courses needed to be scheduled, he was one of the first persons offered the positions. As you can see, it's never too early to prepare and it's impossible to do too much networking. Both of these activities payoff, as it did for Dr. Tim.

The philosophy we emphasize here is your uniqueness and encourages an exploration of your total being in the search for your perfect job or career. We teach that this search is an on-going process subject to the influences of a constantly changing marketplace. We want to help you to be sensitive to these changes and to use them as opportunities for increased growth and learning. In this book we want to empower you with techniques that give you a deeper sense of yourself and greater control over your future. We want to help you enhance your self-perceptions and self-efficacy and become more open to the possibility of limitless potential as you approach the job market.

In some places in this book, we will guide you through an overview of past experiences which highlight your significant events and influences. You will be able to identity both the positive and negative aspects of previous work experiences. The concept of "burnout" and its consequences are explored as well as means of combating it. You are encouraged to review your most personally significant successes and accomplishments, both work and non-work related. You want to recognize the multitude of skills, abilities, and special knowledge which you have demonstrated throughout your life. This recognition is enhanced by asking others what they see as skills and abilities you may not notice as special because you took them for granted.

As you review your past and expand your self-concept, you can develop a list of factors which provide a framework for a specific job/career seeking strategy. These factors include values and purposes which you feel gives your life meaning and measurable goals which serve as a guide in your job search. You will also want to identify your: transferrable skills, special knowledge(s), salary range, level of responsibility, working conditions, employment location, and types of co-workers. This list of factors provides invaluable information once you have prioritized them. The pathway to effective job/career change then becomes more focused and the sense of direction more defined.

As your job/career search strategy takes shape, this book will offer you techniques for discovering what Richard Bolles, author of *What Color is Your Parachute*, calls the "hidden job market." Since an enormous number of all jobs are never advertised, individuals who know where and how to look for these hidden jobs have a definite advantage in getting their ideal job/career. This book will teach you to use information interviewing as one technique to develop a network of contacts who can help you find openings before they are advertised. Once your targeted job/career has been identified, it will be easier to write an appropriate creative resume that assists you in securing the specific position you want.

One of the most continually helpful things you can do is to form a support group of one or two people who can offer you encouragement and compliments. These individuals may also be seeking employment, but that is not required. What counts is that they care about your efforts to find your ideal job/career.

Contingent Work (also known as Casual Work)

TEMPORARY JOBS BECOMING A PERMANENT FIXTURE IN U.S.:

Many corporations are discovering a great way to cut costs is to add more and more temporary positions to their workforce while laying off full-time workers. This gives the employers an opportunity to eliminate medical and retirement benefits, which are usually standard with full-time permanent employment. There are other names for contingent workers, namely: freelancers, independent professionals, temporary contract workers, independent contractors, and consultants. Workers in these types of positions know, or should know, that these are temporary positions with limited job security and even less opportunity for career development. This current condition that is sweeping America is cause for alarm. **It reinforces the fundamental concepts of our message which is: you must have plan B (alternate sources of income) and you must be in charge of your earning potential.**

> *"You can have everything in life you want, if you will just help enough other people get what they want."*
>
> \- Zig Ziglar

Securing Your Career Is a Process Not an Event

Upon finishing your masters or doctorate, you can use this career guide as your opportunity to find out how to earn an excellent income.

This book offers you in-depth insights about what steps you need to take to find your ideal job and start on your career path.

These tips will include how to overcome many of the common problems in your job search to find the employment you want. These tips will also provide you with the opportunity to assess all of your skills, learn how to post your resume, and even choose the right career path for you based on your strengths and assets!

This will allow you to sort through many of the opportunities in the job market to fine tune and select the best choice for you. This is going to save you a lot of heartache in working at a job that is not right for you, because these insider secrets will allow you to choose the career path best designed for your skills and preferences!

Within this book we will also discuss what types of jobs are available to people in both the business world and academia so that you can know what opportunities are accessible to you in the job market. The truth is that you can find the job that you have been dreaming of, but you need to know how to look for it, and how to maximize your potential!

Now that you have earned your masters or doctorate, here are a few simple tips to learn how to maximize your efforts to greatly influence your future income.

A New Thinking Approach

WE ARE PROPOSING that you take on a new thinking approach when you consider future jobs or careers or ways to create the lifestyle you want. Dan Pontefract, in his book ***Open to Think: Slow Down, Think Creatively, and Make better Decisions,*** offers a number of things you can do. He suggests 10 Essential Guidelines for Open Thinking. These can easily be applied to your quest for a better more fulfilling life.

1. *Take enough time and be comprehensive.*
2. *Avoid over thinking. After considering your options, be decisive.*
3. *Never make a decision just to say you made a decision.*
4. *Keep flexibility in your thinking.*
5. *Make a list of your best ideas and let your creativity take over.*
6. *Become systematic and organized in all you do.*
7. *Take time to become balanced through min-vacations and meditation so that new ideas can emerge?*
8. *Look for more information so you can properly analyze and evaluate things.*
9. *Be focused. What are the conditions you want to attract?*
10. *Allow time for dreaming , and deciding every day.*

Chapter 2

THE WORLD OF WORK IN AMERICA IN THE 21ST CENTURY

"Opportunity is missed by most people because it is dressed in overalls and looks like work."

– Thomas Edison

DANIEL GOLEMAN, PH.D. in his book, *Working with Emotional Intelligence*, stated "People are beginning to realize that success takes more than intellectual excellence or technical prowess, and that we need another sort of skill to survive - and certainly to thrive - in the increasingly turbulent job market of the future. Internal qualities such as resilience, initiative, optimism, and adaptability are taking on a new valuation." We have to agree. These characteristics that Dr. Goleman suggested are so prophetic and crucial now in order to survive and have the income and lifestyle we all cherish.

The work-a-day world today in America is like no other time. Now American workers are competing with workers from all over the world, and while, private companies are purchased and reorganized and in some cases eliminated. Government programs and researchers are many times discontinued. Developing technologies and economic changes in many cases contributes to transitions such as: job loss, job reclassification, job limitation, and also job creation. With all of the circumstances developing throughout the world as well as in the United States, the landscape of employment for now and the foreseeable future is uncertain and chaotic.

Transitioning to New Employment

Integration of knowledge is critical when moving to new employment. Roger made the transition from high school classroom teacher, to virtual online teacher, to part-time college instructor, to full-time university professor. So it can be done. In another case we met Joe, who owned a motorcycle repair shop in San Diego. To our surprise after a brief discussion, he told us that he was trained and educated as a nuclear medicine doctor. He had always enjoyed riding and repairing motorcycles in his free time away from the hospital. When he discovered a shop for sale, he jumped at the opportunity to be self-employed and own a motorcycle shop.

Foreign Competition

Yes, the world has gotten smaller with the advent of the internet and factory relocations. You have to accept this fact of employment life. Many people in other parts of the world have the same or similar skills and knowledge you have and are willing to work for less money. In addition, many American companies that do manufacturing have relocated their factories into developing countries. The net effect - less jobs available for you here at home at all levels of management and support positions (advertising, customer relations, employee assistance, benefits processing, etc.).

Companies Downsized and Take Over

There was a time when all you had to do was to work hard, be honest, and be dependable. If you did those things, you would have your job for as long as you wished. In recent years, the corporate philosophy has changed to some degree. Many companies decide it is good for their business to eliminate or combine various departments or segments of their operation. The net result: jobs are lost.

Larger companies buy out and take-over/sell-off smaller companies. This has been done many times. One example: A glass manufacturing company in a small town in Pennsylvania had been family owned and successful for three generations. Almost everyone in the town worked for the company. The founders of the company decided to sell it to a large corporation. A week after the sale transaction was finalized, the new management team announced that the company would close. The operation moved to Mexico as part of a Macedonia glass plant. The result was that everyone lost their jobs.

New Technologies

New electronic innovations such as iPads, iPhones, and others have accelerated communications to the point of almost instantaneous technology. This essentially changes the game plan. There is no need to rely on mailing out letters and résumés. We are establishing ourselves with a global presence, if we want to, in which employers can be anywhere in the world. Caution must be taken not to assume that there is no need to have good face-to-face communication skills. A few years ago, William was looking for editorial support for a series of articles he was writing. He posted his request on eLance.com and received responses from individuals in the United States, as well as places like the Philippines, South Korea, and Hong Kong.

Governmental Bankruptcies

Many cities across the United States have declared bankruptcy in recent years and many more are on the brink of bankruptcy. Many states are in financial crises and they may very well have to declare bankruptcy also. What these developments mean for the job search person is that governmental employment does not necessarily mean security. Until recent years the thought that cities and states would go bankrupt and could not meet payroll was unthinkable. What these developments mean is that each of us must have multiple options for employment. The full-time job for today could be eliminated or become part-time tomorrow. The part-time job today could develop into full-time employment in the coming years.

Corporate Bailouts, and Mergers, and Layoffs

Consider the effects of these recent corporate bailouts: Bear Stearns, $30 billion; Fannie Mae/Freddie Mac, $400 billion; American International Group-AIG, $180 billion; the auto industry, $25 billion; Citigroup, $280 billion; and Bank of America, $142.2 billion (Source: www.propublica.org). All of these bailouts occurred during 2008 and 2009. These companies were all mega corporations that most people thought could never fail, but to avoid a devastating economic crash, the government had to bail them out. How comfortable can the average employee feel when the largest organizations cannot survive on their own? I hope you can see from these events that one cannot count on even the best of employers to continue to function and pay employees their wages. We all have to become more self-reliant and have multiple options in place to secure our financial futures.

The Amazon.com Phenomenon

You may remember in the early days of Amazon.com. They sold exclusively books: both new and used. Now they sell just about anything you can imagine that is available in your local department or grocery store. They now have their own trucks to deliver packages. They have started leasing aircraft to move packages more quickly from hubs to local areas. With these changes in how Americans buy and receive their merchandise, there is high risk that many stores will be closing. Individual stores just cannot compete. What is the likelihood that a customer could go into a Macy's store, look through the merchandise and find exactly what they want, And then, pull out their smart phone and order it from Amazon.com at a much reduced price? They would know color, size, fabric, and brand because they just tried on the garment. Other online companies are modeling their approach after the concept that Amazon started. These changes are significant in how Americans buy and receive the products they want. There are predictions that a number of large malls with hundreds of stores are closing or scheduled for closure in the near future. If this doesn't cause you personal concern about your prospects for employment, it should. This is another reason why you will want to have multiple sources of income - including passive income.

There are many opportunities for you to find the right career and income-producing venture. It takes in-depth research.

The World of Work: Things, People, Ideas

Advanced degrees at the masters and doctoral levels open doors and opportunities to you that are not available without these degrees. You put in a great amount of effort, time and money to achieve your advanced degrees. You want to remember that this makes you special. This makes you qualified for certain jobs that you would not otherwise be qualified for.

Things, People, and Ideas

All work can be divided into a combination of working with things, working with people, working with ideas, or working with any combination of these three. You will want to know of these three types of work, which one you prefer. Although in all jobs you work with a combination of things, people and ideas, most jobs require you to focus on one of the three. For example, teachers work primarily with people. Although, as they teach their specialty they are exchanging ideas. They may also be required to use a computer. Obviously a computer is the thing. So teachers primarily work with people, and they also work with things and ideas.

Work For Others, or Work For Yourself or Other Choices

The first issue you want to identify for yourself is where you feel most comfortable. Working for others or working for yourself. When you work for others, you typically have a job that pays an hourly, weekly, or monthly salary. When you work for yourself, you're only paid for the services and products you sell. This is critical that you understand which of these two major realms you are most comfortable with. When you work for others you are generally guaranteed a salary, benefits in the form of medical or dental coverage, paid vacations, and some kind of retirement program. We would estimate that over 80% of all workers work for others. When you work for yourself, also known as self-employment, you usually provide a service, or if you own the business, you provide products. With the masters and doctorate degree there many more options available to you. Self-assessment requires you to understand your special knowledge abilities, skills, interests, and preferred work environment.

Many workers consider only the two ways of earning a living that we just mentioned: an employee or self-employment. There are two other options to consider proposed by Robert K. Kiyosaki in his book, *The Business of the 21st Century*. You may have heard of him through his fabulously successful *Rich Dad Poor Dad* book series. He suggests business ownership and investing as other ideal ways to not only bring home a paycheck, but ultimately become financially secure and even wealthy. So his concept of working includes four choices: (1) *an employee*, who primarily seeks security; (2) *self-employment* where the primary focus is independence; (3) *owning a business* where one attempts to build wealth; and (4) *investor* to create financial freedom. Becoming a business owner today is easier than ever because of a relatively new approach to business called *network marketing*. There are many corporations that offer this way of earning a living. Since there are number of books available on network marketing, we won't go into details here. The important thing about this approach is that you own your own business and it takes an extremely small amount of money to get started. Investing is another possibility for a career and again there are numerous ways to invest, such as, real estate, stocks, bonds, and intellectual property.

We would like to add a few comments about investing in intellectual property. When you think of all of the books and articles you have read throughout your graduate studies toward your masters or doctoral degree, you have no doubt developed an expertise in one or more topics or subjects. Publishing one or more books based on your knowledge is easier than it ever has been. Until recently, to get a book published you needed an agent and most new authors had difficulty obtaining an agent. Traditional publishers are investing a lot of money, time, and effort in a new unknown author. That is no longer the only option. The new way of publishing your intellectual property as a book is through what is now known as on-demand publishing. There are numerous publishers in the country that specialize in these types of publications. When the retail giant, Amazon.com, forms its own on-demand publishing division known as **www.createspace.com**, you know that this type of publishing must be valuable and appeal to a large market. Today everyone wants instant everything and they want instant information. **Google.com** tracks all requests for information and many times books on specific information is not available. Therefore, the option of on-demand publishing is the answer.

If you wrote a masters thesis or doctoral dissertation, you are an expert on the topic of your research. This document can easily be converted into a publishable book in the matter of a few weeks. The cost to do this is almost nothing, if you publish with www.createspace.com. That's why it was created: to give those with special knowledge an opportunity to share what they know with tens of thousands of people around the world. Many of these books are translated into different languages. All of this activity is your way of receiving income from your intellectual property. If you think small for a moment, how many papers have you written in graduate school? A research paper of 20 pages could easily be expanded when you include your point of view and opinion, which is always an option for an author.

In addition to publishing books, you can earn money from your intellectual property through creating videos, CDs, DVDs, and webinars. It does take a little tech savvy and maybe bringing in specialists to help with the implementation of this approach, but the content is yours. Think about this: if you could write a book based on your dissertation, could you write other books based on other areas of interest? Maybe sub-sections from your dissertation are worthy of the subject of a book or DVD. What we are trying to do here is to expand and stretch your way of thinking about employment so that instead of only considering being an employee working for someone else or even being a self-employed person working for yourself, you consider business ownership and investing as legitimate careers. In today's world, there is so much uncertainty and so much opportunity. The landscape of our country is changing rapidly just as the business world is changing at lightning speed. So we encourage you to consider all your options: employee, self-employment, business ownership, and investing.

Special Knowledge

Special knowledge can be considered the areas or discipline percentage, life-long areas of interest such as hobbies and activities. Over time there are many people developing special areas of knowledge through their own reading or free time activities. If any special knowledge is near and dear to your heart, you are looking at career opportunities in this area special knowledge. If you wrote a masters thesis or a doctoral dissertation, you developed special knowledge and expertise in one or more areas. You no doubt did a lot of reading of many articles and books. In addition to reading so much material, you analyzed what you read. You selectively focused on material for your purposes in your document. In many cases you collected the data through interviews, surveys, and questionnaires. You have a great wealth of information that you can apply to your future income-related activities. It's interesting that many times we develop this great expertise, this great knowledge for our academic studies and then we just walk away from it as if it had little meaning other than to help us complete our academic degrees.

Skills and abilities

Now let's look at your abilities and skills. These have more to do with behaviors such as speaking skills, reading skills, and computer navigational skills, to name a few. You'll notice that these three abilities and skills can be applicable to wide variety of jobs and careers, but you have many more. It would be a good idea to make a list of all the ones you possess such as: listening, problem solving, creating, helping others, writing, organizing, etc. Richard Nelson Bolles in *The New Quick Job-Hunting Map* lists numerous skills and traits to help you identify the ones you have.

Work Environments

Where would you like to work? In an office or school building? In a laboratory? Outdoors? You want to know your preferred work environment. The obvious choice too often would be to work inside the building, or outside with mobility throughout the community. Many jobs and careers offer you opportunities to do both. Although one of these is usually primary, knowing yourself in this area is critical to understanding your options.

Jobs/Careers - Always Changing

The days when a job or career last a lifetime are over. In grandfather's day when he was hired he assumed that he would keep that job until he retired. As the world has been shrinking through the Internet and new electronic communication devices, competition comes from everywhere.

In the last few years because of this increased competition, worldwide workers have to assume that jobs and careers are ever-changing. New skills are required. Knowledge is required. And a new attitude toward your job or career is required. This new way of thinking must be implemented in order to have a satisfying and financially stable career.

Graduate Degrees

Masters and doctoral degrees require many skills, abilities and special knowledge which many people underestimate as good value when applied to jobs and careers. In order to complete any graduate degree skills such as reading, research, writing and most of all critical thinking are necessary. These talents are easily applicable into the work-a-day world. Many times those seeking employment underestimate the value of their graduate education. Some people even apologize for their degrees. This is unfortunate. If one is honest with themselves and applies what they learned in graduate school, they can see how they can adapt to a new job or career or another way of earning income.

Open Doors and Opportunities

A graduate degree many times can open doors and lead to new opportunities. It is useful to look at your graduate degree as if it was a union card, giving you access to certain positions that you would not be otherwise able to accomplish. An example of this is teaching at the college level. Almost all academic subjects require the instructor or professor to have a minimum of a masters degree. Although your academic degree may open new possibilities for you, it is hardly ever the only criteria employers look for when hiring. They are looking for the complete package: education, experience, personality attributes and characteristics, and certain licenses and/or credentials.

Downplaying your qualifications

If your situation is such that you are applying for a position that does not require an advanced degree, you may be prudent to not mention your degree. This is politically smart because you do not want to have to defend your rationale for applying for a job below what your education would expect. We only recommend you downplay qualifications if you must apply for a job that does not require a high level of education. Generally, that strategy is a temporary one. Later, you may not feel so desperate and have more time to seek positions comparable to your level of education.

Chapter 3

ALL ABOUT ME

"When you are inspired... dormant forces, faculties, and talents come alive, and you discover yourself to be a greater person by far than you ever dreamed yourself to be."

Patanjali

Some Questions You Should Ask Yourself Before Seeking a Job or Career Change:

1. **Will this position result in a significant improvement in my employment status?**

    Very often we find ourselves so disheartened by our current employment situation that we believe any new job would be better. That is not always true. In fact many times what we really are doing is making a parallel job change. Unless you're sure that the new employment will make a big difference, it would be better to wait a while and do some investigation.

2. **Will it broaden my experience and build my marketable skills?**

   Believe it or not, many jobs that look good on the outside are really dead-end jobs. Built into the job are limitations. I (Bill) recall a discussion with Fred, who was an Emergency Medical Technician (EMT). I asked him how he liked what he was doing and I was surprised when he said he was just about at the limit of what he could do in his profession as an ambulance driver. I asked if there were ways to get promoted into something more challenging. He said, "no." He said that the job would certainly increase in pay as his seniority increased, but as an EMT he was limited to what he could do to help patients in crisis. He said he would need to go to school for additional training and get certified as a para-medic. Then he could use more advanced skills and earn more money, but as an EMT he was limited.

3. **Are the organization's values similar to my own values?**

   You want to be knowledgeable about the organization so that you feel confident their policies and procedures are consistent with your own. One good way to learn about them is to talk to current or past employees. Do your homework and find out all you can about your future employer.

4. **Will I get along well with the people for whom I will have to work?**

   Doing some detective work can pay great dividends. After all, you are planning to spend a minimum of 40 hours a week working for this new organization. It would be nice to feel that it will be an enjoyable experience being around them.

5. **Does it seem that this organization is one for which I would want to work for five years or more? For the rest of my life?**

   This question has a lot to do with what you're expecting from your new employment. Is it a stopgap? Is it something for the short term or something you are hoping to stretch into a long-term affiliation?

6. **Is the salary satisfactory now?**

   The answer to this one can be difficult depending on the type of organization you are considering. Most governmental and public employment jobs like schools or hospitals include the amount of the salary in the announcement of the position. Private corporations and independent businesses rarely announce the salary in advance because everything is negotiated and the salary is one of the biggest ones.

7. **Will the anticipated salary one or two years from now be satisfactory?**

   Predicting the salary can be difficult if not impossible in many cases. One exception that we can think of would be a teacher who is hired with a bachelors degree and plans to get a masters degree as soon as possible for one simple reason: The salary scale for teachers almost always shows the Masters level teachers made more than those with only a BA or BS degree. The Internet allows you to gather data on so many things that just a few years ago was next to impossible to obtain. Do some serious research about many or all of these questions. You can do them indirectly through the Internet, or you can do them directly by contacting those that you believe have the information you're seeking.

8. **How much confidence do I have that I can contribute substantially to this company/organization in the position involved?**

   We believe that confidence is developed through life experiences. One cannot get confidence out of a book or even out of academic courses, but one can gain confidence by completing a difficult course or a difficult degree program. When I (Bill) work with doctoral students to coach them through their dissertations, I constantly see examples of very talented people who for some unknown reason question whether they can complete it. On the other hand, I've met many average to good students who just believe that they will finish their dissertation and graduate. The more you know about the organization you're considering and the more you know about your own talents and abilities and motivations, the easier it is to project how well you will do when you're hired at a particular organization.

9. **Is the position itself interesting and challenging?**

   Too often we have met individuals who seem to only care about the salary and benefits. This is a huge mistake because if one is only motivated by money, sooner or later boredom sets in and we realize that what we're doing doesn't fit our talents and abilities. When this happens we tend to lose interest in our job and just go through the motions to collect a paycheck. All jobs today have job descriptions which are usually written in behavioral terms. If you pick up a copy of Richard Bolles' Quick Job Hunting Map that we mentioned earlier, you will see hundreds of behaviors, special knowledges, and talents commonly required for numerous positions

10. Is a geographic location satisfactory to me and my family?

The location of employment is very critical because you have to decide commuting time, the neighborhood, and consider traffic for the area. A willingness to relocate into a new area also becomes an issue that you want to have clarity on. In Southern California it is not uncommon for individuals to commute an hour and a half to 2 hours to their job site. This could mean getting up at 4 o'clock in the morning and not returning home at the end of the day until 7 or 8 PM. The long-term effects of extended commuting can be extremely negative on an individual's physical and psychological well-being as well as having an adverse effect on family life.

11. Are there desirable community, cultural, and religious facilities available?

Too often jobseekers only consider the corporation or the position without considering the community they would live in and work in. You need to feel that your work world and your non-work world are integrated. You will want to feel that the community you work and live in is the kind of community that has cultural events and activities that are consistent with your values. Of course, maybe the biggest issue of all is safety. What parts of America are safe today? It used to be we only heard of major crime in the big cities. Unfortunately that's not true any longer. So the decision on where to work and what jobs to pursue may be the primary focus of your employment hunt, but there are other considerations which are equally important.

12. **Is this industry expanding and growing?**

    This is where your research skills and ability to integrate knowledge comes into play. Fortunately the Internet now gives you access to data with the click of your mouse. There are millions of websites that represent corporations, governmental departments, and both public and private organizations. There are tens of thousands of blogs and private websites that individuals have created for the main purpose of communicating information. As such, if you are able to remember the ways you started collecting research for all those term papers you wrote in graduate school, the same approach can be used for identifying the future trends for just about any industry. If you wrote a masters thesis or doctoral dissertation you will remember these fundamental parts of your document: statement of the problem, purpose of the study, research questions, as well as methodology. By applying this fundamental approach to any industry or business, you could accumulate an enormous amount of high quality information that could help you with your personal decision-making regarding the industry you are investigating.

13. **Are there other factors causing me to be looking for a new position likely to exist in this new organization?**

    You will want to do a self-assessment of the conditions and factors that are leading you to want to leave your current job or career. Maybe it's low salary or minimal opportunity to increase your salary. Maybe it's the lack of promotion opportunities. Are you experiencing bullying, overtly or covertly? Is your place of employment too far from your home, which requires you to do extensive commuting? For many people, they are just burning out of their current job. Maybe you have lost interest in what you're doing. Organizations change and sometimes they change quickly. So what was a pleasant work environment for you is now filled with stress and high demands. If you have identified a potential employer, one of the easiest ways to find out about that organization is to visit the facility. Talk to employees as much as possible. Always complement them about the atmosphere and the attitudes of those who work there. You will be surprised how often, when people receive a compliment about their job or organization, they are quick to dispute or possibly cast doubt on your perceptions that this is a wonderful place to work. Here again, you have an opportunity to match up your preferences and needs with what you perceive is available in a potentially new work environment.

14. Do I have any opportunity to bargain for salary and/or responsibilities in this position?

You never know if you can negotiate a salary and responsibilities for the job until you ask. If you have an attitude of "no fear," you may be surprised to discover that you could receive a greater salary than initially thought and even negotiate the details of the duties and responsibilities. If you have done a thorough job researching the organization, you may already know that there is a wide range of salaries and benefits. In governmental agencies, including public school districts there are usually pay scales based in part on educational level and years of service. In these cases there is nothing to negotiate because salary and responsibilities are usually locked into an agreement with a union. The best opportunity for negotiations are with private businesses and organizations.

If you take the time and conscientiously research the answers to these questions, you will be in a great position to make an ideal decision on the next step in your employment life.

Personal Characteristics

You are unique. You are special. You have a combination of characteristics that no one else has. You want to be clear on what your personal characteristics are. If you don't have clarity on these what you can do is ask yourself questions. What do you care about? What behaviors do you enjoy doing? By understanding your personal characteristics you can more easily decide which jobs or careers would be best for you. When it comes to personal characteristics, realize that it's important to include as many personal characteristics that you have as possible. It's that combination of personal characteristics that you take with you wherever you go. And you certainly bring it to the employment environment.

In Marsha Sinetar's book *Do What You Love, The Money Will Follow*, she presents a powerful premise that when we devote ourselves to activities that we genuinely love and care about, we will be more successful. When this concept is applied to employment, our financial situation almost always will improve. It's very easy to work harder and to devote more time to our employment when we sincerely love what we do. I, William, for the last 28 years have had the honor and the joy of working with doctoral students assisting them with coaching, consulting, and editing their doctoral dissertations. It has been a joy and a labor of love.

Be Open to New Information

Since our society is moving and changing at what appears to be the speed of light, it only makes sense that you must pay attention to new facts, ideas, and concepts as you become aware of them. You must be open minded and constantly give serious attention to changes occurring in the world. There are Internet websites by the tens of thousands that are devoted to endless topics. And all this information is available for free. We just have to type in the topic and we will get all the information we ever dreamed of. We love books. And we are constantly searching Amazon.com and Barnes & Noble.com for books on topics that are outside our direct area of occupation.

Integrate Knowledge from Various Sources

I, William, was recently observing an interview with a top educator/entrepreneur (Dr. Sidney Harmon, the Executive Chairman of Harmon International and University-Wide Chair at the University of Southern California), who made a strong point that many CEOs of corporations are in daily fear that someone will discover that they only know about their own specific field such as accounting, engineering, or marketing. They are totally unfamiliar and relatively ignorant of other associated disciplines and fields. Our education and focus sometimes funnels our interest into just one area. This can lead to problems.

You must be trying to integrate information and knowledge at all times so that you see how all aspects of life and work are inter-related.

Be Willing to Have Multiple Jobs

My friend, Rev. Dr Jordan Detzer, who was a retired Methodist minister was teaching part-time at Mesa Community College many years ago. He was also teaching part-time with Chapman

University at the Naval Training Center in San Diego. He was teaching for both schools for a number of years and an excellent instructor, who always received high student evaluations. Eventually Chapman University decided that the **distance learning centers**, such as the Naval Training Center, would have full-time faculty. Jordan was selected to be one of the few full-time faculty in San Diego County. After about six months he decided he no longer needed to work at Mesa College. And for the next 15 years he was the top full-time faculty member for Chapman University in San Diego County. This is an example of how multiple part-time jobs can eventually develop into one full-time job. Although Jordan was retired as an active pastor in a church, young couples sooner or later discovered that he was a minister and approached him to see if he would be willing to minister their wedding vows. One of many reasons for their interest in having Jordan officiate their wedding, was that he was willing to go to the beach, or to the mountains, or to the deserts all over the West Coast because these couples had their own special venue where they wanted to be wed. Jordan was always ministering to others even in retirement and that attracted these young couples requesting him to marry them.

Understand the Value of Integrating Your Areas of Knowledge

Be honest with yourself and become an expert on the topics that interest you. Find out what is most important to you. Consider your values and what type of information you can share with others. Then create or seek employment in those areas, write books or give lectures on these topics. This kind of flexibility can also make you very in-demand and employable because you can do so many things well. People will contact you because they can depend on your knowledge and skills to successfully do the job or answer their questions.

See How Different Aspects of Your Background Can be Used in Multiple Domains

Try to do more than one job in multiple domains based on your experiences and background. In addition, tailor your job(s) to yourself, not yourself to your job(s).

Network, Network, Network

It is important to network because when you help people first, at some time or another, they will help you. In addition, they will always have something good to say about you to others. This helps to create a positive reputation. In addition, the use of technology is beneficial and you can use various communication tools to network such as social networking websites, email, chat, instant messenger, and video conferences.

In his fascinating and insightful book, *The 100/0 Principle: The Secret of Great Relationships*, Al Ritter suggests that we take full responsibility for how our relationships are developed and maintained and expect nothing in return. This approach is valuable in all our relationships. Imagine what it would mean when used with potential employers, co-workers, business associates, colleagues, customers, and clients.

Most people looking for jobs will make the contact and complete the application and stop right there. The difference maker is the person who calls back and acknowledges the time the interviewer took to meet with them. Send a thank you note. Show 100% commitment to building a relationship with the contact person or the interviewer.

Chapter 4

Attitudes for Success

"Sometimes our light goes out but is blown again into flame by an encounter with another human being. Each of us owes the deepest thanks to those who have rekindled this inner light."
— Albert Schweitzer

It is Easy to be Nice

BEING LIKABLE ALMOST always makes a positive difference. We've all heard it said, "Treat others like you would like to be treated." The benefits of being nice are not always apparent. But in the job search world employers want employees to get along easily.

Kindness Always Pays

What you want to remember is that you're always meeting people and sometimes your kindness to these people that you don't know pays tremendous dividends. David Topus in his book, *Talk to Strangers: How Everyday Random Encounters Can Expand*

Your Business, Career, Income and Life, he makes the point that these seemingly random meetings can lead to employment. He presents the strategy that validates the idea of the importance of kindness to others. People want to be around other people who are kind and considerate, and always wanting to be helpful. This approach that David Topus suggests is an ideal way to build your network. The larger your network, the more opportunities you have. This concept of kindness validates the popular saying, *"People don't care what you know, until they know that you care."*

Let's face it: people know people who know people. When we show we care for others, we are really also conveying our values. Many times we have read an article we have found that could help someone. Or maybe we have discovered a web site that could be useful to an acquaintance or a friend. It is so easy to pass this information along to them.

The More You Help Others Get What they Want, the More You Will Get What You Want

This is a philosophy that I have heard preached in various corporations such as the Amway Corporation. The commitment here is to give as much assistance and service as you can to other people. This will always open doors to new opportunities, new acquaintances, who probably will want to return the favor. You help them and they will no doubt want to help you. The help they offer may only be giving a name or offering a tidbit of advice. We never know for sure how valuable this advice will be. The bottom line of course, is that we are setting up a process by what we give to others may come back to us from some other source. Giving service to others also creates long-term bonds.

Always Read, Read, Read- There is no difference between those who cannot read and those who do not read; neither of them reads.

In today's instant gratification society, everyone wants all the answers right away. Unfortunately this is not the way things really work. There have been thousands and thousands of excellent books and articles written about jobs and careers. Of course we cannot read all of them, but we can read some of them. Without knowing it we internalize much of the wisdom, insights, and strategies from those books and articles. As we look around we see many people who are super successful. They did not become successful overnight. Their success was based on years of good habits. One of which was reading inspiring and motivational materials. When we read anything, what we are doing unconsciously is creating a silent conversation between us and the ideas and thoughts of the author. We are consciously or unconsciously asking ourselves questions. How does this apply to me? Will this idea work for me? Who do I know that has additional information about a job opening? We are constantly analyzing and critiquing the relevancy of the materials we read. The next step of course is to take action.

You may have heard or read this frequently quoted saying, "Knowledge is Power." We would like to offer an improved version, "The appropriate application of knowledge is power." Knowledge without action is just interesting.

Take Time for Silent Time by Using Meditation and/or Prayer

Meditation and prayer have been part of human society for eons. Regardless of what we call it, meditation and prayer are important. The beneficial aspect is to take time, relax, and open our minds to inner knowledge. We all know what to do, if we would only listen and pay attention to our inner selves. The meditation process that Bill likes to use is to sit in a comfortable chair with eyes closed and take a few deep breaths and mentally tell each part of his body to relax and let go. Starting with the face and going through all parts of the body, he mentally commands all parts of his body to relax. This creates a subtle and yet powerful calming effect. This phase of relaxing all parts of the body may take as much as 10 minutes depending on how specific you are in mental directives. After all of his body has been relaxed, what he likes to do is to repeat his own private mantra that he chose for himself. You can pick the statement - a phrase or a word you like best. You can repeat this word or phrase silently in your mind over and over for as long as you choose. The length of time for your meditation is not so important. What is most important is to meditate as often as possible.

Regular meditation opens us up to our inner knowledge that we all have and helps to make our decisions and actions more effective.

Preferred Work Environment

What preferred work environment do you have that you need on the job? Do you prefer to work indoors, such as an office? Do you prefer to work outdoors? Do you prefer mobility? Do you prefer the freedom to make choices regarding what you do, where you work, and how you perform the required duties and responsibilities? Do you need the freedom to choose the details of your work assignments?

Too often people take jobs they are qualified to do but the day-to-day requirements of those jobs do not integrate with their own personal characteristics and needs. As an example, consider the position of a fifth-grade teacher. One could teach in a self-contained classroom where the teacher is alone with the class of 22 students. At another school the fifth-grade teacher does team teaching with two other teachers working with possibly 60 students. Would an individual be equally comfortable working in both classroom environments? For some teachers it would not matter. For others, they would not feel good about working in a classroom with other teachers. So the personal characteristics and preferences you have will make a difference on the job.

We suggest that you make a list all of your preferred work environments. Knowing these will make it easier for you to predict your level of satisfaction and comfort in a new position.

Chapter 5

Maximizing Yourself

Constant Job Searching

TIMES HAVE CHANGED. The days when a person could get a job and keep that job for lifetime are just about over. With competition for jobs higher than ever, and so much pressure from workers in other countries, you are not competing only with other American workers, you are competing with workers around the world. Therefore, you are going to have to change the way you think about jobs and careers.

A few years ago a friend of mine, Fred, constantly applied for jobs posted. He did this on a regular basis and tried to submit a new application every week. This was before there was so much competition for jobs from other countries. He didn't wait until he was laid off because he said he didn't want to risk being out of work. So his approach was to be in a constant mode of applying for jobs believing that a new job better than the one he had was out there. This approach of constantly applying for new positions pays off. When he started this constant job searching behavior, he was an administrator in the school district. He found out about a position in acquiring land for a major corporation that built utility lines across America. His new job allowed him to travel throughout the areas where the new utility lines were planned and to identify potential landowners who would be willing to sell or lease their land to his corporation. He's much happier now and he earns about twice as much as he did when he worked in education. The concept of constantly searching and applying for new jobs is a new habit for most Americans. What does this require? It requires regularly visiting job websites, paying attention to postings, actively listening to those people in your personal network for possible positions. You are going to want to have more than one resume. Maybe even three or four. Each resume tailored for particular type of job or position. You are going to want to have a separate cover letter applicable to each resume. Let us give you an example from the field of education. You could have one resume that focuses on teaching in public schools, a second resume devoted to your qualifications to teach at a community college, and a third resume that summarizes your preparation and validation to teach online college courses.

If you are unemployed this process will work just as well. Let's look at areas other than education. You could consider three different categories of work (1) management, (2) sales, and (3) technical. These three areas are common in the business world. It never hurts to be creative regarding how you promote and discuss your qualifications for a position. Today more than ever, employers are seeking the best-rounded, flexible, and multi-talented candidates.

Regarding the resume that is geared to management, you will want to consider presenting your areas of expertise, people skills, problem solving skills, understanding of their field and the business.

When creating a resume that focuses on possible sales positions, you will want to put the emphasis on your communication skills, your ability to work as part of a team, and your knowledge of the company's product or service. A lot of individuals, including the authors of this book, shy away from sales. Many times it's because we do not understand how sales works in many corporations these days. Much of sales today are really managing accounts of existing clients through regular customer visits to encourage the client to continue to use the products or services and to identify potential problems before they occur. Another aspect regarding sales positions is the surprising variety of education and diverse backgrounds many people have. For instance, for many pharmaceutical sales positions, individuals are hired with degrees in communications, history, political science, English, or psychology, even though these positions require knowledge of the drug and a knowledge of how the drug works in the body. These pharmaceutical companies are looking for personable individuals with excellent communication skills, who they believe can be trained to understand the details of the products they represent when calling on physicians.

Many people believe it is desirable to have only one great job. However, one has to think if this is a wise choice. In today's economy individuals need to think about Plans B and C, regardless of the security of their primary job. No one really knows if the company they work for will have to cut back or reorganize; so it is important to explore your options. In order to prepare for a potential job loss, you can make a smooth transition into your next job by constantly improving your skills, staying current with technology, making sure you network with people and send out your updated resume to specific people. Also, it is important to constantly update your curriculum vita/resume so that you can keep track of the job skills you have gained.

Some people who have earned their masters degrees and doctorates have more than one job. This does not mean that they work full-time at all of their jobs. For example, many have a ground-based job and also work online doing the same or different types of work. However, having more than one job can require good organizational skills and time management in order for it to be effective.

OVER-QUALIFIED: You may have heard of the term, "overqualified." This is used many times to dismiss candidates because the employer believes they could never hold this employee very long because they have too many executive type skills that are not required for the current job. You will want to be cautious when applying for jobs or moving toward a career where it is somewhat beneath your present abilities. This issue of over qualification came up for William when he was the director of an education center in San Diego for Chapman University. In those days we had administrative assistants and since the academic curriculum was primarily for teachers getting a masters degree and nurses getting their bachelor of science degree, we were in need of a very competent staff. William recalled hiring Marilyn, who was a doctoral candidate at Kent State University. A number of my colleagues criticized his desire to hire her because she was so called "overqualified." Indeed she was. What Bill appreciated about her was her unique ability to relate to all the students. She had already been through what our students were going through in the bachelors and masters programs. She had accomplished what they were doing educationally. She was employed for two years. And I know she added quite a bit to the program even though she was "overqualified."

Evaluate What You Have: Your Skills, Abilities and Special Knowledge

Evaluate what you can do in terms of skills, abilities, and special knowledge. Richard Bolles' book, *What Color is Your Parachute?* has been revised and published each year for about 20 years and is probably the second-most published book in America. The Bible may be number one. Bolles talks about knowing your own various skills, abilities, and special knowledges. He has a very profound way of explaining how you can do this. In the book, he has a section that lists many, many skills and abilities that are clustered. For instance, talking. Isn't that simple, everybody can talk. But think about the various ways that we can talk. We can begin to dialogue. We can give a speech, right? We can counsel or consult. Talking is communicating. What types of communicating can we do and do well? Of the talking that I (Patricia) can do, what do I feel I'm best at? I think I'm best at coaching and advising.

Someone else might say, "well, they think they're best at giving a speech, you see." Bolles gets far deeper than that. These are a few options but the point is that he goes through, oh, I think there must be 100s of categories of things that people can do. And so what he says for the individual to do is to pick six successes. Let's imagine that one success was graduating with their degree. Another kind of success was a certain job. Another kind of success was performing some kind of hobby or outside interest.

So let's get back to what would be the first success, completing their degree. As they look down the column of behaviors, they put a checkmark beside everything they did that's on that list that they used, even once, as they got their degree. They do that, really, for six different successes. Now, remember, he's defining success as anything you've already done. It's like, can you ride a bicycle for two blocks? Yes. Well, then you can probably ride a bicycle for two miles. In other words, you can ride a bicycle, right?

So what Bolles does is get people to self-assess – and this is in the middle of his book, I think he has a separate book called, *The Job-Pointing Map*. But it's the same concept. For people to self-assess what skills, abilities and special knowledge do they have? And it's not just – for instance, I love baseball. Now where's my success in baseball? I mean, I wasn't a minor league player; I wasn't a major league player. You understand? Now, I could choose, if I wanted to, to say my success is a lifelong interest about baseball. So it wouldn't be demonstrating, can I hit the ball, can I pitch the ball? It would be more about baseball, do you understand?

So inside that book, *What Color Is Your Parachute*, by Richard Bolles, I think it's called the *Quick Job-Hunting Map* or something like that, is a separate publication. That would be ideal for somebody, anybody, no matter what age, to do this and assess what they can do. Bolles also has a website that you may find useful: http://www.jobhuntersbible.com/.

And with the idea about picking six successes, you start to see that certain behaviors or special knowledges are used over and over again, in multiple successes.

So that would be one way to take that point, assess what you can do.

You have to target what you're good in and you'll have a lot more fun with finding out what you're supposed to do.

This means taking an inventory of your strengths and weaknesses to determine exactly what you have to offer to your future employer.

Chapter 6

What Jobs/Careers Are Out There?

"To find what you seek on the road of life, the best proverb of all is that which says: Leave no stone unturned."

– Edward Bulwer Lytton

As someone in academia with a doctorate, it is important to know what types of jobs are out there for your job search.

Consider Traditional Employment

With the achievement of earning your masters or doctorate, you have the opportunity to work in traditional on-ground employment. This will include: managers, professors, researchers, university administrators, lecturers, and even college presidents.

Online Teaching

This is something that many instructors use as an additional income, but it also provides the opportunity for full-time teaching after earning your doctorate. This sets you up as an adjunct faculty, and these positions often pay more than traditional teaching positions. This is also something that is quite convenient if you want to extend your job market to anywhere in the country since you will be working online.

Self Employment and Entrepreneurial Employment

As reported in *Entrepreneur*, the United States Census Bureau found that 52 percent of small businesses are home-based.

This is the perfect entrepreneurial employment opportunity, which allows you to own your own business. You can participate in training programs or Internet marketing to deliver your products or services to the customer in your niche market.

My guess is that you are in some way in the idea business: teaching ideas, writing ideas, researching ideas, coaching ideas, or in some other way conveying ideas to others. In this process of idea sharing, you are using your own experience and creativity. And these have value. I'm sure you will agree.

Therefore, I want to share **The Picasso Principle** with you. The story goes like this:

A woman asks Picasso, who was seated in a restaurant, to sketch something on a piece of paper for her. He does, and says, "That will cost you $10,000." Astounded, she said, "You took just five minutes to do the sketch. Isn't $10,000 a lot for five minutes work?" And he responded, "The sketch may have taken me five minutes, but the learning took me 30 years."

We live in the ideas and information age; let's remember the value of what we do.

Coaching/Consulting

Both coaching and consulting have unlimited possibilities. Nearly every industry or business requires assistance from coaches and/or consultants. These individuals are highly knowledgeable and specialized in the services they provide. A simple example is computer and software consultants. Many of these individuals work for corporations and companies, while others work for individuals and small businesses. In many cases coaches and consultants are not required to have any type of license or credential. They have specialized knowledge that they sell for an agreed-upon price. I (William) have a "computer guy" named John who assists me with computer and software problems when needed. He also works full-time at a major corporation in their IT division. We have known consultants who work in such diverse fields as: criminal justice, education, steel manufacturing, accounting, nursing, interior decoration, aircraft maintenance, and travel. These are just a few of the industries and areas where coaches and/or consultants are hired.

If you wrote a masters thesis or doctoral dissertation, by definition you are an expert at some level in the topic of your research. It is very possible that an area of employment is directly or indirectly related to the topic you studied. It would not take much investigation on your part to identify possibilities as a coach or consultant in your field of specialization.

Non-Profit Employment

This is employment for charities, trade unions, and even public arts organizations. Often times, these organizations can cater directly to your area of expertise and study within your doctorate. Your experience can open the door to a position with any of these non-profit companies.

Research Fellowships

This is an alternate area of employment where a research fellowship will be awarded based on specific criteria. These fellowships are often given depending on the needs of the founder/donor, and they can provide an extra source of income for your research.

Chapter 7

Be Strategic About Your Job Search

"Use your gifts faithfully, and they shall be enlarged; practice what you know, and you shall attain to higher knowledge."
—Matthew Arnold

WHEN IT COMES to maximizing your earning potential after completing your masters or doctorate, it is important to be strategic about your job search. You may be surprised to know that there are a number of employment websites that cater to the specific job opportunities listed above, and many more!

These websites can be easily used so you can post your resume, which affords you the opportunity to network by having potential employers always able to access your updated resume. This is even better than searching for a job yourself because your information is out there and available, so **an employer in need can recruit you.**

PostDocJob.com

This website is an employment website for a specific niche market in those looking for postdoctoral employment. This is a recruiting website for professors, research institutions, PhDs, and employers to find what they are looking for. This website offers over 100,000 PhDs looking for postdoctoral jobs, and this site boasts providing employment for research associates, scientists, and recent PhD graduates.

TedJob.com

Tedjob.com is a website that allows you to search for the best higher education jobs on the market. It will help you to do an advanced search based on the keywords that you are looking for and to browse potential employers in your area of specialty. You can also take advantage of the education center on this website that provides information on continuing education for your degree.

Phds.org/postdoc/postdoctoral-fellowships

This is a website with complete listings on postdoctoral jobs, science jobs, research jobs, and other listings in higher education employment. It also offers the convenience of career resources, especially in that of finding a job after earning your doctorate. This website provides information on how to get a job, cover letters, the labor market, and even non-academic careers.

PostdoctoralFellowCrossing.com

This is a gold mine of a website that claims to provide insider postdoctoral job information that you can't find anywhere else. This website takes higher level education jobs from a number of career websites and job boards, including newspaper classifieds. They even boast job postings from Fortune 500 companies. This is a specific postdoctoral website for those seeking jobs, and they do not allow advertising on the website.

AfterCollege.com/job-channel/phd-and-post-docs

This is a career website that has specific listings for PhD and postdoctoral jobs. You can search by keywords or your location, and they also have job categories for full-time, part-time, and other selections. Many of the jobs can also be searched for by the level of experience that you have, whether it is 0 to 1 years, 1 to 3 years, or not specified.

Jobs.Phds.org

This is a job database that has specific job listings for PhDs, and they are also divided by keywords and categories. Within this section, you can search particularly for postdoctoral jobs. Other job options include employee, tenured faculty, non-tenured faculty, graduate fellowship, internship, or temporary employment.

Monster.com

This is a more commercial job listing, but it provides you with a number of resources in postdoctoral employment. Again, this is a job website that will allow you to search for free based on your zip code and area of location. You can search specifically by the "postdoctoral" keyword, and you can also use keywords in your area of study. One benefit to this job search website is that you can look at related job titles in your field.

HotJobs.Yahoo.com

This is another job source website that will allow you to search by your post doctorate keyword. It also provides information on the top 100 companies available, and it allows you to set up a job watch for yourself based on what you are looking for in your career.

CareerBuilder.com

This website will help you to search for jobs in your area of expertise, and it also will provide information on posting your resume online. You can directly post your resume for a number of employers to view, depending on their needs. This website will also send you job alerts when a job that fits your qualifications is available. There are a number of categories in the job search available, and you can also search by company.

SimplyHired.com

This job search database will allow you to search by keyword and location, and they also claim to have the biggest job search engine online. This website has advanced tools to allow you to identify trends in your area of specialty, and you can even research the salaries that are available to you.

Job Search Tools

Employment Trends

This is an interesting tool to look at to determine what is needed in the job market. For instance, when you type in "post-doctoral" at **http://www.simplyhired.com/a/jobtrends/**

trend/q-postdoctoral, you can see a simple chart displaying increase in postdoctoral jobs since April 2008. The great news for you to know is that postdoctoral jobs have shown a steady increase by 113% at this time! You can enter even more keywords to find out greater information about the employment trends in your field.

Career Assessment

At **CareerPath.com**, you can access a Free Career Assessment, which will allow you to input your skills and knowledge, rate your own skills, and enter your own experience and personal information to find the jobs that are right for you. If you're having an issue with getting started on your resume, then this is exactly what you need to do to determine your strengths and weaknesses, as well as your area of expertise.

Resume Writing Service

Monster.com also has a resume writing service available, and it even provides resumes for professionals and executives. This is your opportunity to impress employers who are hiring to show your full value. If you just don't know where to begin when it comes to your resume, this is a helpful tool to use.

Calculate Your Salary

If you are hoping to maximize your potential income after earning your doctorate, then it is best to calculate your potential salary right away. This will help you to decide which fork in the road to take on your career path if you have several decisions before you. This tool can be found at **HotJobs.Yahoo.com**. It allows you to input a job title and location to determine how much you can earn in your area. It is important to know what the competition is asking for so that you understand that the salary they are offering is appropriate.

Chapter 8

INTERVIEWING TIPS

Be Able To Identify Your Skills

EVERYONE HAS SKILLS and abilities. It is important to know and be able to discuss what those are so that we can intelligently talk about ourselves during the interview to impress upon the interviewer regarding our potential value to the organization. Many career counselors advocate that each person memorizes a 3 to 5 minutes personal commercial for ourselves so that whenever the interviewer asks a question such as, "Can you tell me about yourself?" it is easy to discuss what we see as our special skills and abilities. It's not enough just to know what these are, it's also important to know the context or the job situations that these skills and abilities are used in. Richard Bolles in his book, *What Color is Your Parachute?* claims there are 4,341 transferable skills. He lists a few dozen which are separated into numerous skills and abilities broken down into various sections. Bolles, also suggests that the reader list six accomplishments, successes, or jobs that they've had in the past. And for each of these note the behavior, skills, abilities, and special knowledge you used.

I (Bill) can recall when I was hired as a center director for Chapman College at George AFB many years ago, there was a tradition for the director of the program to make a brief speech at a Commander's Call once a month to greet all the new airmen that had recently been assigned to the base. My only previous experience at giving speeches was when I took a required speech course as part of my bachelors degree. I was surprised when my supervisor said that I needed to give a speech that day in front of around 200 airmen of all ranks regarding the programs and credentials that were available at the Chapman College program on base. It was difficult and I'm sure I did a poor job that first time. But I noticed that the more I presented those brief speeches at Commander's Calls, the more confidence I gained in my speech-making abilities. A few years later, I was able to conduct trainings in various parts of the Southwestern United States regarding burnout prevention and intervention. Sometimes the skills and abilities we have are latent and forgotten only to be rediscovered. Yet it's only after we try again that we see firstly, that we have the skill or ability and secondly, that we are capable of using them competently.

Being able to intelligently and confidently discuss our skills and abilities will go a long way during the interview process to impress the interviewer regarding our potential value to the new organization.

Be Able To Quantify (Validate) Your Skills

Within a job interview, the odds are that you are going to be asked about what you have contributed in your past employment. You need to be able to explain in detail how you have built successful teams and carried out your skills in the workplace. Make sure that you have references available for these statistics, and that they are noted on your resume.

Dr. Mary G. was a clinical psychologist living in the Chicago area. This is what I wrote to her after reviewing her curriculum vita. She was applying for a position as a college provost at a private university…

"It is great to hear from you. Your career is going well and I'm glad to know you are applying for the college provost position."

Here are some on my perceptions and feedback regarding your curriculum vita:

- *When relevant and irrelevant entries are mixed, the reader generally will not take the time to analyze everything;*
- *You may want to edit your vita to include only those items pertinent to the provost position so that you have 2nd specialized «administrative» vita in addition to your «regular» vita.*

A cover letter is critical to gaining the attention of the decision-makers and needs to be crafted in such a way that you make a strong case for yourself. What skills, abilities, attributes, and experiences do you have that are needed to be successful as provost? What experiences and education/training validates your claims?

You will want to be very knowledgeable about the present challenges and circumstances the college faces. Then offer a hint about the direction you would take to address these conditions.

I hope these points are helpful."

Discuss How You Contributed To Past Employment Success

The more specific that you can be, the better. It is important to be able to discuss in detail how you have developed any processes or results in your past employment for the greater success of the company. This is something that is quite impressive to the interviewer because it shows that you could provide the same results to their company. Another example from Bill in which he was able to show the successes he had as a college administrator, was when he claimed that he founded and developed the first civilian education center for Chapman College (now Chapman University) in San Diego County. I was able to explain that I started a program for registered nurses to earn a BS degree in health science and placed that program in eight hospitals which were sent throughout the county. This degree program was brand-new and no other location within the job and college system had developed a successful BS in health science program.

Prepare Yourself for the Interview!

When it comes to your job interview, make sure that you prepare yourself well. It is important to know the name of the person that is interviewing you so that you can use it within the interview process. It is also essential to do your homework on the company that is interviewing you so that you can sound intelligent when they ask you the inevitable question of why you want to work for their company.

Not only do you want to be able to be knowledgeable regarding your position you're applying to, but you want to be able to intelligently discuss the competition. Now with the Internet putting out information as public knowledge, so many aspects of just about every organization is available. There's no reason for a person to apply for a job and not have at least some knowledge of the company they are applying for. There's also no reason to not know other similar companies, organizations, and what jobs are available there, where they're located, and how they're different from the organization they're currently applying to.

Dress Professionally

This seems quite obvious, but it is important to dress in professional business attire when undergoing an interview. This is something that will set you apart as an expert, and it will also impress the recruiter interviewing you. It is important to wear appropriate clothing to the company or business that you are interviewing with.

My friend, Michael and I were teaching a course in San Diego many years ago we were doing a roundtable discussion using brainstorming techniques to identify possibilities for jobs and careers. An attractive woman in her mid-30s had made comment to the group that she was continually passed over for promotions within the electronics company that she worked for. She was wearing a red dress somewhat short and I guess most people would say she was dressed in a voluptuous manner. Before Michael or I could respond to the possibilities regarding why she was not getting promoted, another one who had been working in the bank wanted to comment. This woman asked the question of the first one, "The way you're dressed now, would you say is the way you dress most of the time on the job?" The first woman said, "Yes, I try to look nice."

The second woman made comment that although she is an attractive woman and does dress nice, she appears to be dressed in such a way that she is promoting her femininity too much. She suggested that the first woman dress in a more conservative manner. This way management at the electronics company would focus more on her skills and abilities and less on her attractiveness.

This is a delicate subject and rarely discussed. Certainly her supervisors would be hesitant to address the style of clothing she usually wore to work. This woman wanted to be acknowledged and promoted for her skills and abilities, but unfortunately the image she was projecting was not appropriate.

Always Be On Time!

There is nothing more discouraging than someone being late to an interview. If you want to set yourself head and shoulders above your competition, then make it a priority to be early to your interview to impress your prospective employer. This is a simple thing that will set you apart.

Use Your Knowledge

It is best to demonstrate the understanding you have of the company that you are interviewing with by integrating this knowledge into the way that you answer questions. For instance, if the interviewer is asking you what your strengths are, you can relate them to the specific needs of the company, showing that you have an understanding of the job opening you are interviewing for.

Be Prepared to Talk About Yourself

Interview questions may seem absolutely daunting, but there are a few questions that you can prepare for to stay calm. First of all, be prepared to be asked to tell about yourself. This should relate more so to your work skills than your personal home life. Take this opportunity to discuss your past career path, and how it relates to the job that you are now applying for.

Discuss Your Strengths

This again seems like another trick question, but you most likely will be asked to discuss your strengths. The best way to use this question is to again subtly advertise yourself because no one else will do it for you. You can take this opportunity to talk about your organizational skills, ability to handle numerous tasks, or capability of staying calm under pressure.

Discuss Your Weaknesses

This may seem like an intimidating question, but you do need to be prepared for it. This is a question that you will absolutely want to think through because you don't want to reveal that you are lazy or short tempered. It is better to use neutral weaknesses, like being too hard on yourself or becoming impatient with coworkers who do not share the workload.

Have Questions Ready at Your Interview

Again, this is something that you should be prepared for because you most likely will be asked if you have any questions about the company that you are interviewing with. This is your opportunity to put the homework that you have done into action to ask specific details about the structure of the company or position you are applying for. It is not a good idea to use this time to ask about raises, but instead to discuss the inner workings of the company itself.

Project Your Future Goals

You may also be asked where you see your career in 5 or 10 years, which can be a tricky question. You don't want to seem as if you are temporarily working at this company to get to the next rung on the ladder, and it would be a better answer that you see yourself moving up within the company that you are interviewing so that they can determine your longevity and commitment.

Discuss Your Skills

You will be most likely asked to discuss any skills you have that would benefit the company that you are interviewing with. These skills should be keywords that directly relate to the job posting to show your qualification for the position. Again, do your homework and look over the job posting to make sure that you can use exact keywords and qualifications for the needs of the company.

Discuss Your Past Employment

This may be another question that is cause for alarm if you are asked why you left your last job. Do not use this opportunity to trash your former boss or coworkers, but instead attempt to remain neutral and speak of looking for a more challenging position with more job responsibility. It is better to leave out conflicts or issues that may have happened in your past job because they will be a red flag to your potential employer.

Chapter 9

Tips for an Impressive Resume/Vita

Writing a Cover Letter

IN SOME WAYS your cover letter is more important than your resume/vita. How is this possible? For one thing, the cover letter is shorter which makes it easier to read. Secondly, it is personal. It is addressed to the reader. Thirdly, the cover letter addresses the specific position. And fourthly, it is highly focused on the specific skills and experience applicable to the job.

The Arizona Republic in their "azjobs section" suggested five tips for writing a cover letter, which are critical in making a good impression:

(1) Avoid "Dear Sirs;" (2) Name the job; (3) Proofread; (4) Don't be generic; and (5) Don't challenge. If you address your letter to "Dear Sirs," you are assuming the only a man will read it. How

would a woman feel when reading it? My guess – it could be thrown in the trash or misfiled on purpose.

Before You Even Write Your Resume

On top of that, it is so necessary to have a base resume that you can customize to every job opportunity. This is something that will impress employers to no end, so take the time to carefully read each job posting to determine what the employer is looking for. This is also your opportunity to use the keywords found within the job posting to relate directly to your strengths. This is something that will immediately catch the eye of the employer when you use some of the exact wording found in the job posting on your resume.

As an example, if the employer is looking for a candidate that excels in "critical theory and practical training," then you can use **those same keywords on your resume**. This may seem like a subtle difference, but it is the way to tailor your resume exactly to your job posting to present yourself as the best candidate.

Within the next chapter, we will discuss resume writing and posting tips.

Post Your Resume

There are a number of job posting sites available online, which is your opportunity to post your resume that you have tailored to each specific job opening. It is necessary to put yourself out there and use keywords within your resume to customize the resume to employment opportunity.

Higher Ed jobs.com and a few other places hold your resume so that you can easily apply to jobs as they come up in your field. They are a holding tank for you and it is convenient to apply to different universities when they offer the subjects and opportunities in your field. When it comes to resumes, there are two kinds. There is a general, all-inclusive resume, and then there is a specific resume for one type of job or career. For instance, if someone only wanted to teach in higher education they could create a specific resume that focuses just on their academic background and/or special training. Whereas, a general all-inclusive resume would include the most recent to oldest job experience.

We recommend including your most recent job experience first. If someone has a doctorate in Education, the first under Education would be, Ph.D., Education, University of –, and mention the date. Under Education, if a Ph.D., for instance in Education is not as spicific to those who review your resume. They would need to review your core courses or specialized courses in that degree program. You do not have to list all of the courses, but some of the major ones. It is recommended to have more than one resume depending on what you do and your experience. In addition, it is important to send the right resume to the specific school or institution.

One of the things you have to be careful of is that you cannot assume that people read resumes the way they read a book. We think most people skim and focus on what they think they want to find. To us, it is the cover letter that goes with the resume that makes the difference. An impressive cover letter is going to be very focused. It will show why the resume is being sent to whomever and how it is related to the job or position. Moreover, it will provide important points about your background and experience. It can specifically support your qualifications for a job or specific career. A resume should never be without a well-written, very focused cover letter, and is related to this job or that position. Then, in addition to that, the applicant is going to point out things in their background. Hopefully, it's also noted in the resume, that what they believe specifically supports their qualifications for a job or specific career. Resumes and cover letters go together. A resume should never be without a well-written, very focused cover letter.

Write Your Resume to Get Results

This may seem like a no-brainer, but you need to write your resume in a way that will generate the most results in your job search. There are many factors to take into consideration, like the objective of your resume, your format choice, the sections of your resume, and your resume tone.

Use Your Resume to Pass the Screening Process

This is the number one reason to customize your resume for every job because it must pass a screening process. Many companies use resume screening software, which is another reason to use keywords from the job post. There are also a number of minimum requirements that your resume could be screened for, like your education level, years of experience, and even location in the US.

Remember Your Contact Information

When formatting your resume to pass the screening process, you must remember to include your contact information. This would be an up-to-date phone number and address that you can be reached at. Often times, if this information is not available, your resume will be immediately thrown out. Remember to ask colleagues or employers for excellent recommendations only.

Only have High Quality Writing

Again, this is probably a no-brainer, but it is so important to use high standards in writing your resume to establish yourself as a professional. Basically, your resume needs to be clear, well-written, organized, and printed on quality paper. If you are someone who specializes in writing or design in your area of study, your resume can also be a direct example of those skills in the way you create it.

Avoid Making Your Resume Your Personal History

Your resume is a summary of your skills and strengths to show the direction of your career path. It is a mistake to include on your resume your personal statement, history, or autobiographical information. It is a definite no-no to ever include your height, weight, marital status, or ethnicity on your resume.

The Resume Is Used to Sell You!

The main purpose of your resume is to provide a quality product, *which is YOU!* This is your opportunity to subtly advertise yourself and your skills on your resume, which happens directly in how you word the resume itself. For instance, instead of stating that you can type a certain number of words per minute, you can word that information in a way showing that you are an advanced typist at X number of words per minute with certifications in computer training and online teaching. Much better!

Declaration and Confirmation

The two main components of your resume will be your declarations and confirmations. This seems simple enough, but your declarations will take the opportunity to assert your qualities, achievements, and abilities. These statements do need to be honest, and they can powerfully advertise what you have to offer. From there, you will back up these declarations with confirmations and evidence of the truth. This shows your job experience, education, and credentials to support your skills.

Focus On Your Declarations as These Apply Directly to the Position/Job

This is the most important part of the resume, and you can use your declarations to entice the prospective employer to want to know more about you. These declarations should be written in such a way to showcase your best skills and excite the potential employer. Even better, it is best to leave some mystery in what you write so that whoever reads your resume will be wanting more, leading them to call you in for an interview.

Have Multiple Versions of Your Resume to Target Different Positions/Jobs

This is very significant because it shows clarity in the direction of your career. This will be found in the objective section of the resume to state your intention and direction in your job search. This will set your resume apart from many generic resumes from people who are just sending them out on the off chance that they will get called in for an interview. Your objective needs to be purposeful to show clear direction in the position you are applying for.

Your Cover Letter Needs to Focus on the Applied Position

This is also an important portion of submitting your resume to a number of employers. One of the first things to consider is the appearance of your cover letter. Keep in mind that a potential employer may see hundreds of qualified applicants, and it makes an impression to use a higher-quality stock of paper, perfect grammar, and a simple font.

Choose a Simple Font

Even though you want to stand out from the pack, it is better to go with a basic font on your resume. This will make it easier to read for yourself and the HR department. The area that you will want to stand out in is in your skills, not necessarily the font chosen for your resume. In this case, less is more. We recommend New Times Roman.

Suggested Organization

As a basic rule of thumb, it is better for your most recent experience to be listed first on the resume, as well as your most important accomplishments at the top. This is an important organizational tactic that will draw attention to what skills you are hoping to show to your employer with your resume. List in this order: education, experience, credential/licenses, honors.

Ensure Accuracy!

This should be something that goes without being said, but allow a friend or family member to meticulously check over your resume. There is nothing more embarrassing than sending out a resume and cover letter with grammatical errors that you did not catch in the first place. This is something that could cost you a potential interview because it is a careless mistake.

Cover Letters and/or Email Messages

Do not ever send out the same cover letter to all employers! It is so important to format your cover letter for each resume submission; otherwise, your cover letter and resume may be thrown out immediately because they are generic and cookie-cutter. It will be quite obvious if you are using the same cover letter for all job applications.

Clarity is Critical

You can easily go too far with your cover letter by using big words that you may have substituted with the use of a thesaurus. Make sure that your wording in your cover letter is something that you would also use in conversation. It will look suspicious if your cover letter is heavily worded with text that is meant only to be impressive.

Celebrate Your Uniqueness

It is important to use the text in your cover letter and resume showing that you are truly one-of-a-kind. This will set you apart in the mind of a prospective employer, and it also will show that you have more to offer through your area of study in your doctorate. This is your opportunity to do so on your resume so that the potential employer will be attracted to the special skills that you possess.

Be Persistent

The job search after earning your doctorate may or may not be as easy as you anticipated it to be. Continue to submit your resume to the area of interest that you specialize in, and don't give up right away if you don't get the first job that you want! That is the beauty of using online job search websites, because they allow you to continue to submit your resume to a number of employers with more access than ever.

Be Open to Revising your Plan

That being said, if you are continually hitting dead ends in your job search, then it may be a good idea to reassess what type of job you're looking for. Maybe you have completely overlooked a lucrative career path that is in demand. Rethinking your goals will allow you to continually assess if you are heading in the right direction post doctorate.

Research Unmet Needs

SHARON'S STORY: Being a single mom with a four-year-old daughter, Sharon had a Masters degree in counseling and no job. She decided to investigate something as simple as bookkeeping. So she went to 10 small businesses and met with the owner or manager of each one and asked a few simple questions: Who does your bookkeeping? Who keeps the records? Who does the payroll?

She was surprised to discover that in most cases the owner or the owner's wife did the bookkeeping and they didn't care for this role. She had already investigated what bookkeeping firms charge on an hourly or project basis and she knew she could offer the same service at a reduced fee with more personalized attention. Within a few weeks she had over 32 clients. She called her service Peppertree Bookkeeping. After two years of providing this service for her clients, she approached each of them and offered a new additional service which she called *business consulting* related to the amount of inventory being purchased, where advertising monies were spent, as well as suggestions on newer better ways to find and retain employees. About 10% of her present clients have decided to hire her for extra business consulting services.

One of the best things that you can do for yourself on your post-doctorate job search is to be hyperaware of the job market out there. The best way to do so is to research what type of needs are not being met in the job market. You can also do this through numerous websites. This will allow you to slip into an opening when it presents itself, potentially landing the perfect job for you.

You are unique with special preferences and skills. Never settle for the first job that looks appealing without first investigating the details of the work environment. You can easily do this when you talk to employees. Complement them and their company or organization. When you do this you trigger candid feedback from them most of the time. This way you will probably receive the greatest insights into this particular organization you are considering.

Be Careful Where You Post your Resume!

Overall, you need to take the opportunity to post your resume to a number of sources to put yourself out there after earning your doctorate. Again, all resumes must be customized to each specific job or position, but it is important to submit your resume to a number of sources online and otherwise, which we will discuss in future chapters.

Here is a sample of a post-doctoral resume of a person interested in consulting found at http://www.vpul.upenn.edu/careerservices/gradstud/postdocresume.pdf:

MARY K. NAME

123 Home Street

City, ST 11111

(2xx) 555-1212

name@server.com

**SAMPLE
OBJECTIVE**

Position in management consulting. State-of-the-art knowledge of biotechnology. Experience working in teams of international researchers. Ability to communicate complex concepts to many audiences.

**SAMPLE
EDUCATION**

University of Pennsylvania, Philadelphia, PA, Biomedical Graduate Studies February, 2003

Ph.D. in Molecular Biology

GPA 3.9/4.0, Phi Beta Kappa

NIH Training Grants: Cell and Molecular Biology, 1994 to present, Genetics, 1988-1991

University of Massachusetts, Amherst, MA May, 1995

B.S. in Botany, *cum laude,*

SAMPLE
RESEARCH EXPERIENCE

University of Pennsylvania, Philadelphia, PA

Postdoctoral Fellow 2003 to Present

Ph.D. Candidate 1997-2003

- Researched gene encoding and DNA sequencing.
- Oriented new researchers to lab, while acting as part of team whose members came from four countries.
- Supervised work of graduate students, including one whose work was published.
- Worked with senior researcher to write successfully funded grant for $750,000.
- Ordered equipment for new lab and established guidelines for its use.
- Research resulted in joint authorship of nine publications in scientific journals and five presentations at national and international meetings.

SAMPLE
TEACHING EXPERIENCE

University of Pennsylvania, Teaching Assistant, 1999 and 2001

- Chosen to deliver lectures and prepare course materials for graduate course (2001).
- Graded exams and prepare materials for first-year graduate courses (1999).

SAMPLE
LEADERSHIP

University of Pennsylvania

Genetics Seminar Committee 2002

- Selected and invited outside speakers for student-run seminar series.
- Organized speakers schedules.

Molecular Biology Graduate Group Admissions Committee 1999-2001

- One of two student representatives elected to serve a two-year term.
- Reviewed and ranked several hundred applications to the graduate program.
- Organized outings for visiting candidates.

(Specialized or focused Format)Sample

Chapter 10

Networking

Create Allies

THIS IS THE perfect form of networking, and it means creating contacts and friends in a number of fields. These are people that can give you insider tips on openings within a company, specific advice on what an employer is looking for, or even guidance on how to look for jobs within a specific market.

Complement Others' Careers

Take the opportunity to find out what others are doing in your career field of choice. This will provide you the opportunity to complement these careers by choosing something similar on the same path. By finding out more information about colleagues or people working in your chosen field, you can also find out information about jobs in your career path you may not have known about before.

The next topic would be networking and that would include complimenting others on what they do best or just the way they look, showing interest in others, including their families—showing interest in other people's interests.

I mean, I don't care about golfing, but if someone I want to foster a relationship with likes to golf, I can at least inquire about when do they golf, where do they go, how long have they been golfing? What do they like about golfing? In other words, I'd want to get them to talk about golfing. It draws them to me, so that our relationship can have some meaning. You can build rapport.

Yes, build rapport. Let's call it developing relationships. I guess that's the outcome of networking. All are important.

They are and they can lead to future jobs for a person. I think I've had more than three connections where I've actually gained from that. Meeting one woman, my friend Judy, a colloquium for the Ph.D. program, led to me adding about $40,000 a year to my income. Just by acquiring the one University. And it's because I networked with her and it was very light talk. We're not great, great friends, but we're good acquaintances and we get along real well. I'm (Patricia) in education. She's in business and in management, but somehow, we had the commonality of majoring in the same subject, which is post-secondary and adult education. So we had something to talk about. When she received a job promotion, she said, hey, let's schedule you for training. I had been trying for two years to get into a certain University and she scheduled me right out and I got two or three classes, four classes now. Additionally I was selected for a pilot program and now they're sending me more opportunities for a leadership position.

You know, one fundamental thing – and I don't know if Richard Bolles brings this up – I believe it in my personal experiences and I know I've read in other places – in selecting people for jobs, the public responds to why was so-and-so selected, because almost always, they were the most qualified. And that has to be the public stance. But the real truth is, a lot of people have similar qualifications, why was so-and-so selected.

And it gets back to likeability. They were liked best. In other words, getting back to you as an example, you had tried the formal approach to getting a teaching position at the University. It was only when you had established a networking relationship with somebody, who knew of you, who met you, liked you, okay, and then still, you had to have the qualifications, you had to have the educational level, the experience level that they were looking for. But again, your name meant something when the hiring person is deciding to hire or to refer you to maybe the Dean or someone else. So it's that personal connection that made the difference. And ultimately, I'm sure everybody who applies to teach, if you look on paper, they probably have similar degrees.

If a doctorate is required, then they all have doctorates.

Network! Network! Network!

When it comes to looking for a job in your field of interest, it is important to make contacts and do networking. Part of that includes developing relationships to make connections within your field. You can do this by showing interest in others' families, talking about their interests, and developing relationships. This will afford you the opportunity to get to know people, who may later provide you with an open door to a job opportunity.

Build Your Reputation

One of the best things that you can do for yourself is to establish yourself as an expert. Who doesn't want to hire an expert? You can take your area of study or specialization in your doctorate and begin to build upon that. This could be in the form of continuing education, certifications, and gaining further experience in your field. If you have the opportunity to learn or do something that no one else in your field can, you can achieve expert status.

Now what did we mean when we say, Build Your Reputation?

I think that kind of feeds into Developing Relationships, too, because I believe your reputation ties into that. If they know you, they like you. You've got to have a pretty clean reputation, too, once they know you. It's a small world out there, and names go around. So I think it's important to keep your reputation as clean as possible.

You're talking about formal – in other words, not getting into trouble with the law, am I right?

And you're also talking about just the way we treat people.

You know, it's interesting. I would say a certain percentage of my clients just have what I would call almost a disrespectful,– I don't know what else to say –

A demeanor or just their approach? Yes, it's their demeanor. Their approach is like, oh, you're just there. I'm hiring you just to help me. In other words, I don't really care about you in any way, shape or form, other than the knowledge that you give me or the service that you can provide for me. And then there are people who are the opposite way. They treat me like a person. I am a person. I want to be treated like a person. I want to treat them like a person. And, to coin a phrase of one of the businesses in San Diego County, "it's so nice to be nice." There's nothing wrong with being nice. In fact, nice makes a difference.

It makes a big difference. Along with developing manners. If you don't have manners, try to improve in that area.

Counsel and Coach Others Who May Need Your Expert Help

There is no better way to learn further than by doing, which is what coaching and counseling offers you the opportunity to do. Since you have your expertise and specialty through your doctorate, you can learn more and build up even more skill through coaching and counseling others who may need your help.

Where are we going to do that? I think that has something to do with what we talked about before, with servant leadership. I think it has to do with helping others attain success. And in doing so, we kind of attain success, too, because we're helping others. When people succeed around us, we tend to get some of that and we benefit. So we are talking about being willing to help others, even if it's nothing more than listening to their issues and problems. We can offer sincere insight or sincere solutions such as letting others know about helpful books for websites. And we can make that something that we do as part of our life. When we have an opportunity to help someone, to step up and just say, 'Have you thought about this?' It is not so much that we're insisting, not so much that they are wrong. It's just that we see things they don't see because they're admitting to us that they have a problem. A lot of the people that we know have financial problems.

I, (William), had a client who said, "Well, gee, I don't know if I can afford to have weekly appointments, because I'm only a part-time professor at this little college. I'm trying to get more work." So he would be someone that would be good for me to let him know about HigherEdJobs.com.

So you're sharing. We're not preaching to these people, but we're sharing. And we're trying to help. Let's focus on that word 'sharing.' Sharing information. Actually, you know what goes with that - listening. How rare that is? Listening and sharing.

Use Online Social Media

Since most of your job hunting will potentially be done online, it is best to become active in online social media networking. There are a number of job forums that you can become a part of, and they will provide you with the opportunity to meet and connect with colleagues and potential contacts.

The websites below are offered as resources to assist you in obtaining information and networking as you gather knowledge and insights to build your career and lifestyle.

Twitter

This is a social media site that has been all the rage in recent years, but it is mainly used by business professionals. People of all ages have Twitter accounts, and many use them to stay up to speed with the latest happenings in their area of expertise. If you are hoping to find information about your job market, there are a number of relevant people that you can follow on Twitter to do so.

Link to Twitter

If you are active on Twitter and LinkedIn, you can have your Twitter feed on LinkedIn. This means that any users on LinkedIn that do not have Twitter accounts can also stay updated with your conversations on Twitter. This is the best of both worlds in merging two social media websites together.

LinkedIn

This is a highly popular social networking site for your career. This website allows you to look for jobs, but even more so, it will help you to establish connections when applying for jobs. One of the best aspects of LinkedIn is that you can create a profile with a picture. This puts more personalization to your resume, and you can also include specific keywords so that employers can find you more easily.

Indeed.com

This website has specific job forums on post doctorate subjects. Some of the questions being discussed within the forums are: how to get a postdoctoral job, tips for postdoctoral interviews, typical post doctorate salaries, and advice from professionals in their post doctorate careers. This is exactly what you need to network and find insider advice!

About.com Job Search Forum

This is another helpful forum that will provide insider information on the online job market. You can come across helpful interview question tips, how to write a resume, and even what to do if you are at a dead end in your job search.

JobForums.org

This is another helpful resource that will allow you to communicate with other job seekers. This forum also includes employers, and now you have the opportunity to interact with prospective employers throughout the entire forum. Many employers use this forum to look for potential employees, which is the perfect example of networking. If you are on this forum, then you may be located for a job opening!

Learn4Good.com

This is a job forum that allows you to find information about employment opportunities. There are a number of resources on this website, including subjects on post-doctorate information.

JobSeekersAdvice.com

This is a career forum that provides information about changing careers, advice on specific careers, employment issues, job hunting tips, and even job posts found online. If you have specific questions about your specialization in your post doctorate degree, then this is the type of forum that you have been looking for.

Build a Network

With the use of Linkedin and other social media websites, it is important to connect with other members. These connections will provide more opportunities on the job market in the form of a business relationship. This does not mean that you need to go overboard and try to get as many connections as possible, as many people do with Twitter, but make lasting and genuine connections that will benefit your career.

Get Recommendations

Many of these job networking sites will provide you with the opportunity to post recommendations from past employers. This is exactly what you need to add more credibility and expertise to your profile online. Take the time to post recommendations to your profile to verify your past career experience.

Plaxo

This is a similar networking site to Linkedin, and you can make your own profile with your contact information. This site also offers an address book for all of your connections, and you can search through a number of employment listings in your area. This is also an ideal networking website to use for employers recruiting for new job positions.

Facebook

Yes, Facebook is incredibly popular for almost everyone on the planet, but it can also be used for the job market. There is the Facebook marketplace, which has opportunities and job openings available. If you find a job that you are interested in, you can send a message directly to the hiring manager to initiate communication. You can also join a number of groups on Facebook to network with people in your career field.

Craigslist

If you are hoping to find job listings off of the beaten path, then Craigslist is incredibly popular. Most of these postings will be for smaller or independent companies at the midsize level. There are new listings posted to Craigslist on a daily basis, and if you visit this site daily, you may have a leg up on the competition in finding a job in your market.

MyWorkster

This is another online networking site through Indeed.com, which brings students and alumni together in a college network. Users cannot access this site if they did not attend college, making it perfect for post doctorate connections. This site will allow you to create your own professional profile to network with hiring employers.

VisualCV

This is a job search networking site that uses personal branding. Instead of uploading your resume, you will have your own webpage. On this page, you can include audio, video, images, charts, your portfolio, and your references. This is an easy way to set yourself apart from the many resumes posted on a number of websites because it will immediately personalize your qualifications. These profiles can be either public or private, and they can also be e-mailed directly to a hiring employer.

JobFox

This is an online job networking site that is more similar to online dating. This website will take all of your information to try to pair you up with the perfect job for you in a matchmaking scenario. This website will intake your experience, skills, and goals to find the right job for you.

Ning.com

This is another online networking website for a number of subjects. This allows users to share social networks, many of which includes job searches. You can access this website for your own area of expertise in your post doctorate studies.

Look for a Specific Company

This is an easy way to use many of these social networking sites listed above, and you can search on LinkedIn for a specific company. This will allow you to connect with other people within the company that you are interested in to make personal contacts.

Link To Twitter

If you are active on Twitter and LinkedIn, you can have your Twitter feed on LinkedIn. This means that any users on LinkedIn that do not have Twitter accounts can also stay updated with your conversations on Twitter. This is the best of both worlds in merging two social media websites together.

Use Blogging

One of the best ways to establish yourself as an expert is with the use of blogging. Your blog is your own opportunity to gain exposure back to your niche and area of expertise. Often times, people online are looking for experts in their industry, and posting regularly to a blog will provide you with the opportunity to generate content to show your knowledge.

Participate in Publications

Depending on your specialty in your doctorate, you can network even further and gain exposure through submitting your work to a number of publications online. This is all dependent upon your area of study, but if you can provide your input, you will often times have much more earning potential because of the knowledge and experience that you have exhibited.

Chapter 11

Concluding Reflections

Success Doesn't Necessarily Depend on Talent

THIS IS ONE of the most important keys to keep in mind because your talent does not necessarily determine your success. The people who have been the most successful do the best job in presenting themselves, having people skills, relating to people, and being likable enough to land a job.

Read About Success

One of the best ways to be successful in your career is to learn by example. You can start and read books about success, like *The Tipping Point* by Malcolm Gladwell, *Talent is Overrated* by Shel Perkins, *The Magic of Thinking Big* by David J. Schwartz, and *What Color is Your Parachute* by Richard Nelson Bolles.

In *The Tipping Point*, the message is that we get to a point in our life where our knowledge kind of leads us where we want to go, our interests leads us. We don't have to be pushing, looking,

looking, and looking. I had a colleague a number of years ago. She was an expert on sex education. She was also a clinical psychologist. Let's call her "Judy." I called her up and said, "Judy, how come you haven't called me and let me know when you're available to teach?" And Judy said, "Bill, you don't understand. I get calls every day for people wanting my services. I don't have time to go looking for work." For her, the tipping point had gotten at that stage, at that point, when all the offers were coming to her. She no longer had to go looking. So she was in demand by numerous schools, by clinics, she was writing two books. So she had gotten to a point in her life and career, where as much business and income was coming her way as she could handle.

And how did she get to that point? It was years. And she did have the credentials. You know, that's the other thing, you have to have it. There are fields where I think academics does not matter. I think of the computer field. There are these computer geeks who just know computers. They live that stuff and whether they have a master's degree in computers or not, they do it, and they know they can. Microsoft is famous for hiring people who are computer savvy with or without the so-called proper education and credentials.

In *Talent is Overrated* the point of that book is that success is not necessarily based on talent. It never hurts to have talent, but talent alone rarely gets people where they want to go. Another great book is *The Magic of Thinking Big*, which has been around for about 30 years now. I love that book because it really opens us up to really thinking about unlimited opportunities.

Build Your Personal Brand

To make your job search even easier on yourself, take the time to build your own personal brand. In his book, *Impressions: The Power of Personal Branding in Living An Extraordinary Life*, Coyte G. Cooper, PhD states, "Personal branding is about building a reputation with the people around you that will allow you to cultivate and enhance relationships that open up opportunities in your life." He offers a number of tips to help create your personal brand. Here are just a few: make the effort to be excellent in all that you do; develop an attitude whereby you add value to those around you; improve your likability; never underestimate the importance of even the smallest activity; conduct daily self-reflections of your activities and skills used; and be natural and confident just being yourself.

Try Googling Yourself

If you are wondering what this has to do with your post-doctoral job search, then it is simple. Googling yourself will allow you to see what type of information is available out there on you. This is the same information that a potential employer would see if they were to Google you, and you can use it to make sure that your press is positive.

Use Your Own Blog to Be a Leader

If you haven't noticed by now, blogs are all over the Internet and these are many people's main source of information. If you have started a blog, you can provide your knowledge on your area of specialty from your doctorate, which will immediately get you noticed. Being able to cite a blog when being interviewed for a position will set you ahead of many other qualified candidates. You would be positioning yourself as a "thought leader," a person who influences others.

Have a Digital Resume On Hand

Since you will be applying for many jobs online, having a digital resume is a must. This will allow you to showcase your portfolio easily, it's accessible to anyone who is hiring. In this day and age, it is necessary to have a handy digital resume to compete with all of the other candidates on the market. This will also allow you to easily link to it from any networking sites that you are part of to showcase your qualifications.

Be a Giver

If you are looking for openings or job opportunities, then giving will equal receiving. It is important for you to be willing to give your time or talent in the form of free articles, guest blog posts, guest speaking, or even your expert advice. This is another way to establish your credibility and reputation to get your name out there in your field.

Use All of the Resources Available

It is important to make use of all of the resources in job search engines, job forums, contacting your university directly, local organizations, word-of-mouth, or even newspaper classifieds. Leave no stone unturned in your post doctorate job search!

Don't Job Hunt at Your Current Job

This is something completely unprofessional that will come back to bite you. If you are online looking for a job or calling prospective employers at your current job location, then that could easily be picked up if your company monitors the Internet or phone usage. Keep your job search and current job completely separate!

Rehearse Your Interview

Of course, you don't want to sound like a robot at your interview, but if you are quite nervous, it is helpful to rehearse what you are going to say with a friend or spouse. This will allow you to get the ball rolling and feel comfortable when it comes time for the actual interview.

Stay Positive

In your post doctorate job search, it is important to stay positive. It may seem devastating or embarrassing not to get the job that you are hoping for, but the worst thing that could happen is for a potential employer to turn you down. That's it! Take a risk and put yourself out there so that you can get the job that you are looking for.

Include Keywords in Your Online Resume

This is essential because if you are posting a resume online, then employers will be able to find you by the keywords that you use. Not only should you use keywords when submitting a resume for a job position, but you should also use keywords based on your qualifications when posting a resume to a job site or social networking site.

Compare the Competition

If you are wondering how you measure up or just want to get some ideas on your job search, then look at some of the other similar resumes that are posted online! Maybe you have been overlooking some skills that you already possess or even keywords within your resume content. Checking out other similar resumes online in your field will allow you to stay abreast of the competition.

Ask For Help

If there is anything that you are confused about, make sure that you get the help you need in valuable online resources! As was mentioned before, there are a number of online job forums, and there are also professionals out there that you can speak with for free or at a small charge. If you are serious about your job search, there is help out there for you.

Consider a Temp Position

If you are looking for employment at a college or university, there is often contracted, temporary, or seasonal work available. This could be the perfect opportunity to get your foot in the door to try out something completely new. Who knows? It may lead to the job that you have been looking for.

Create a Resume Template

This is a simple way to have your base resume ready and on hand so that you can customize it according to any specific job opening. It is important to re-emphasize that all resumes should be customized for each job available so that you can groom all of your skills to showcase yourself for that specific position.

Have Credible References

Nothing holds up your job search more than having invalid references. Many times, if a company cannot get a hold of your references, they will throw out your application completely. Furthermore, make sure that you have credible references to support your online resume and your work history.

Go Local

On top of all of the large post doctorate job search sites within this report, make sure to look at local listings in your area and local job search websites. These sites may provide you with something that you cannot find anywhere else, which is especially convenient since it is in your area.

And there you have it! With the insider tips in this report, you now have maximum potential in your post doctorate earning capabilities! We encourage you to read these tips again and again to make sure you are on the right track in your new career path.

Success is at your fingertips, and you are now more equipped and qualified than ever in your post doctorate job search!

Afterwords

Applying What You Learned

KNOW YOURSELF: What are your specific skills, abilities, and special knowledge?

KNOW WHAT YOU WANT: What kind of environment do you feel most comfortable in? Do you primarily enjoy working with people, ideas, or things? What lifestyle do you want to live?

BUILD A NETWORK: Get the names and e-mail addresses of everyone you know.

CREATE YOUR OWN WEBSITE: This is your window to the world. The perfect way to promote yourself and your projects.

MAKE THE EFFORT: make as many calls and e-mails contacts per day as you can. When we are employed, we work 40 hours a week or more. When looking for your ideal income-producing environment, we need to devote a similar amount of time and effort.

CONSTANTLY RE-EVALUATE YOUR SITUATION: What results are you getting? How are you progressing to where you want to be?

TREAT EVERYONE AS A VIP: You never know when someone will lead you to that magical happenstance that will change your life for the better.

About the Authors

William G. Wargo was the founder and chief consultant since 1990 of the Academic Information Center, Fallbrook and Menifee, California, specializing in coaching, consulting, and editing doctoral dissertations and books for graduate students from over 227 schools and universities. He offered career consulting to graduate students as well as assisting them in converting their dissertations to books and journal articles. He earned his Ph.D. in psychology from United States International University (now Alliant International University). He previously authored *Secrets and Tips for Dissertation Completion* (Lulu Press) in 2011 and has written 37 articles which are posted on the website, www.academicinfocenter.com. He has provided trainings and consulting to numerous organizations including: American Society for Medical Technology; California Department of Motor Vehicles Managers Association; Children's Hospital (San Diego); Clinical Laboratory Management Association; DuPont Corporation; National Student Speech, Language, and Hearing Association; National University; Southwest Wyoming Rehabilitation Center; Union Institute; University of California, San Diego; and University of San Diego. For many years he managed a private practice in career consulting.

Patricia V. Tobin earned her Ph.D. in Education; specializing in Post Secondary & Adult Education from Capella University, a Master of Arts degree in Studio Art from California State University, Fullerton, and a Bachelor of Fine Arts from California State University Long Beach. She is a university professor, curriculum writer, faculty mentor and coach, and doctoral committee member. She also holds a teaching certificate for grades 7-12. Patricia currently instructs coursework at the undergraduate, graduate, EdD, and PhD levels for various US universities and in the United Kingdom. She is a fine artist, researcher, educator, and has authored a number of books and articles. Dr. Tobin's expertise and research interests include student engagement and success, student retention, adult learning theory, career advancement, nontraditional and at-risk learners, faculty retention, best practices in online learning, emerging technology in course design and instruction, online education, learning styles, diversity leadership, servant and transformational leadership. She integrates theory into practice through conducting research in these areas. She can be contacted at patriciatobin@hotmail.com.

www.ingramcontent.com/pod-product-compliance
Lightning Source LLC
LaVergne TN
LVHW051601080426
835510LV00020B/3086